# Holidays In Cross-Stitch

# 1989

## The Vanessa-Ann Collection

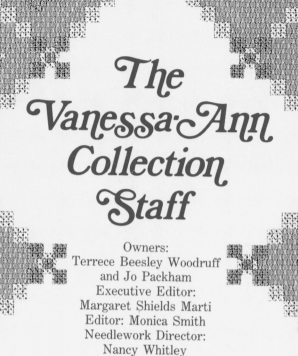

# The Vanessa-Ann Collection Staff

Owners:
Terrece Beesley Woodruff
and Jo Packham
Executive Editor:
Margaret Shields Marti
Editor: Monica Smith
Needlework Director:
Nancy Whitley
Graphic Artist: Julie Truman
Graphing Director:
Susan Jorgensen
Operations Director:
Pamela Randall
Administrative Assistant:
Barbara Milburn
Customer Relations:
Kathi Allred

# Designers

Trice Boerens
Linda Durbano
Vickie Everhart
Barbara Heward
Margaret Marti
Jo Packham
Julie Truman
Terrece Woodruff

# Holidays In Cross-Stitch
## 1989

The Vanessa-Ann Collection

*Barb,*

*I want to be the one—for all of us—to say thank you for everything, but most of all for just being you.*

*We love you. . . .*
*Jo*

Library of Congress Catalog Number: 86-62285
ISBN: 0-8487-0727-3
ISSN: 0890-8230
Manufactured in the United States of America
First Printing 1988

Executive Editor: Candace N. Conard
Production Manager: Jerry Higdon
Associate Production Manager: Rick Litton
Art Director: Bob Nance

*Holidays In Cross-Stitch 1989*

Editor: Linda Baltzell Wright
Assistant Editor: Kim Eidson Crane
Editorial Assistant: Laura Miller Kurtz
Copy Chief: Mary Jean Haddin
Designer: Diana Smith Morrison
Photographers: Ryne Hazen, Colleen Duffley,
  Melissa S. Rogers, Gary Clark, Jim Bathie

Our special thanks to these people for the use of their homes and businesses in the photography of this book: Clyde and Pat Buehler; Nan Smith; Edie Stockstill; Kaysville Library, Kaysville, Utah; Mary Gaskill at Trends and Traditions on Historic 25th Street, Ogden, Utah; Wasatch Floral on Historic 25th Street, Ogden, Utah.

To find out how you can order *Cooking Light* magazine, write to *Cooking Light*®, P.O. Box C-549, Birmingham, AL 35283

# 1 9 8 9
*Contents*

# Introduction

At The Vanessa-Ann Collection, our individualities seem to surface as we plan each new *Holidays In Cross-Stitch* book. This year we celebrate holidays that are sacred and secular, familiar and unique. You'll find novel interpretations of favorite holidays and traditional designs for little-known occasions. In 1989 we're also remembering the bicentennial of Washington's inauguration, the centennial of the Tournament of Roses Parade, and with our French friends, the centennial of the Eiffel Tower's construction.

So choose from the variety of designs and express your talent and individuality through cross-stitch. "Vive la difference!" as they say across the Atlantic. We salute the individuality of each of you in *Holidays In Cross-Stitch 1989!*

# 1989

### JANUARY
| S | M | T | W | T | F | S |
|---|---|---|---|---|---|---|
| 1 | 2 | 3 | 4 | 5 | 6 | 7 |
| 8 | 9 | 10 | 11 | 12 | 13 | 14 |
| 15 | 16 | 17 | 18 | 19 | 20 | 21 |
| 22 | 23 | 24 | 25 | 26 | 27 | 28 |
| 29 | 30 | 31 | | | | |

### FEBRUARY
| S | M | T | W | T | F | S |
|---|---|---|---|---|---|---|
| | | | 1 | 2 | 3 | 4 |
| 5 | 6 | 7 | 8 | 9 | 10 | 11 |
| 12 | 13 | 14 | 15 | 16 | 17 | 18 |
| 19 | 20 | 21 | 22 | 23 | 24 | 25 |
| 26 | 27 | 28 | | | | |

### MARCH
| S | M | T | W | T | F | S |
|---|---|---|---|---|---|---|
| | | | 1 | 2 | 3 | 4 |
| 5 | 6 | 7 | 8 | 9 | 10 | 11 |
| 12 | 13 | 14 | 15 | 16 | 17 | 18 |
| 19 | 20 | 21 | 22 | 23 | 24 | 25 |
| 26 | 27 | 28 | 29 | 30 | 31 | |

### APRIL
| S | M | T | W | T | F | S |
|---|---|---|---|---|---|---|
| | | | | | | 1 |
| 2 | 3 | 4 | 5 | 6 | 7 | 8 |
| 9 | 10 | 11 | 12 | 13 | 14 | 15 |
| 16 | 17 | 18 | 19 | 20 | 21 | 22 |
| 23 | 24 | 25 | 26 | 27 | 28 | 29 |
| 30 | | | | | | |

### MAY
| S | M | T | W | T | F | S |
|---|---|---|---|---|---|---|
| | 1 | 2 | 3 | 4 | 5 | 6 |
| 7 | 8 | 9 | 10 | 11 | 12 | 13 |
| 14 | 15 | 16 | 17 | 18 | 19 | 20 |
| 21 | 22 | 23 | 24 | 25 | 26 | 27 |
| 28 | 29 | 30 | 31 | | | |

### JUNE
| S | M | T | W | T | F | S |
|---|---|---|---|---|---|---|
| | | | | 1 | 2 | 3 |
| 4 | 5 | 6 | 7 | 8 | 9 | 10 |
| 11 | 12 | 13 | 14 | 15 | 16 | 17 |
| 18 | 19 | 20 | 21 | 22 | 23 | 24 |
| 25 | 26 | 27 | 28 | 29 | 30 | |

### JULY
| S | M | T | W | T | F | S |
|---|---|---|---|---|---|---|
| | | | | | | 1 |
| 2 | 3 | 4 | 5 | 6 | 7 | 8 |
| 9 | 10 | 11 | 12 | 13 | 14 | 15 |
| 16 | 17 | 18 | 19 | 20 | 21 | 22 |
| 23 | 24 | 25 | 26 | 27 | 28 | 29 |
| 30 | 31 | | | | | |

### AUGUST
| S | M | T | W | T | F | S |
|---|---|---|---|---|---|---|
| | | 1 | 2 | 3 | 4 | 5 |
| 6 | 7 | 8 | 9 | 10 | 11 | 12 |
| 13 | 14 | 15 | 16 | 17 | 18 | 19 |
| 20 | 21 | 22 | 23 | 24 | 25 | 26 |
| 27 | 28 | 29 | 30 | 31 | | |

### SEPTEMBER
| S | M | T | W | T | F | S |
|---|---|---|---|---|---|---|
| | | | | | 1 | 2 |
| 3 | 4 | 5 | 6 | 7 | 8 | 9 |
| 10 | 11 | 12 | 13 | 14 | 15 | 16 |
| 17 | 18 | 19 | 20 | 21 | 22 | 23 |
| 24 | 25 | 26 | 27 | 28 | 29 | 30 |

### OCTOBER
| S | M | T | W | T | F | S |
|---|---|---|---|---|---|---|
| 1 | 2 | 3 | 4 | 5 | 6 | 7 |
| 8 | 9 | 10 | 11 | 12 | 13 | 14 |
| 15 | 16 | 17 | 18 | 19 | 20 | 21 |
| 22 | 23 | 24 | 25 | 26 | 27 | 28 |
| 29 | 30 | 31 | | | | |

### NOVEMBER
| S | M | T | W | T | F | S |
|---|---|---|---|---|---|---|
| | | | 1 | 2 | 3 | 4 |
| 5 | 6 | 7 | 8 | 9 | 10 | 11 |
| 12 | 13 | 14 | 15 | 16 | 17 | 18 |
| 19 | 20 | 21 | 22 | 23 | 24 | 25 |
| 26 | 27 | 28 | 29 | 30 | | |

### DECEMBER
| S | M | T | W | T | F | S |
|---|---|---|---|---|---|---|
| | | | | | 1 | 2 |
| 3 | 4 | 5 | 6 | 7 | 8 | 9 |
| 10 | 11 | 12 | 13 | 14 | 15 | 16 |
| 17 | 18 | 19 | 20 | 21 | 22 | 23 |
| 24 | 25 | 26 | 27 | 28 | 29 | 30 |
| 31 | | | | | | |

## JANUARY 1
# The Tournament of Roses' 100th Anniversary

Roses are a gentle way to ease into a hectic new year, and Pasadena's Tournament of Roses has more than two million of these flowers. So on the 100th anniversary of this parade, stop and smell the roses. (Wait until tomorrow to think about the 364 days to come!)

# A Bouquet of Roses

**SAMPLE**
Stitched on tan Jobelan 28 over two threads, the finished design size is 7¾" x 9⅝". The fabric was cut 14" x 16".

10

**Stitch Count: 109 x 135**

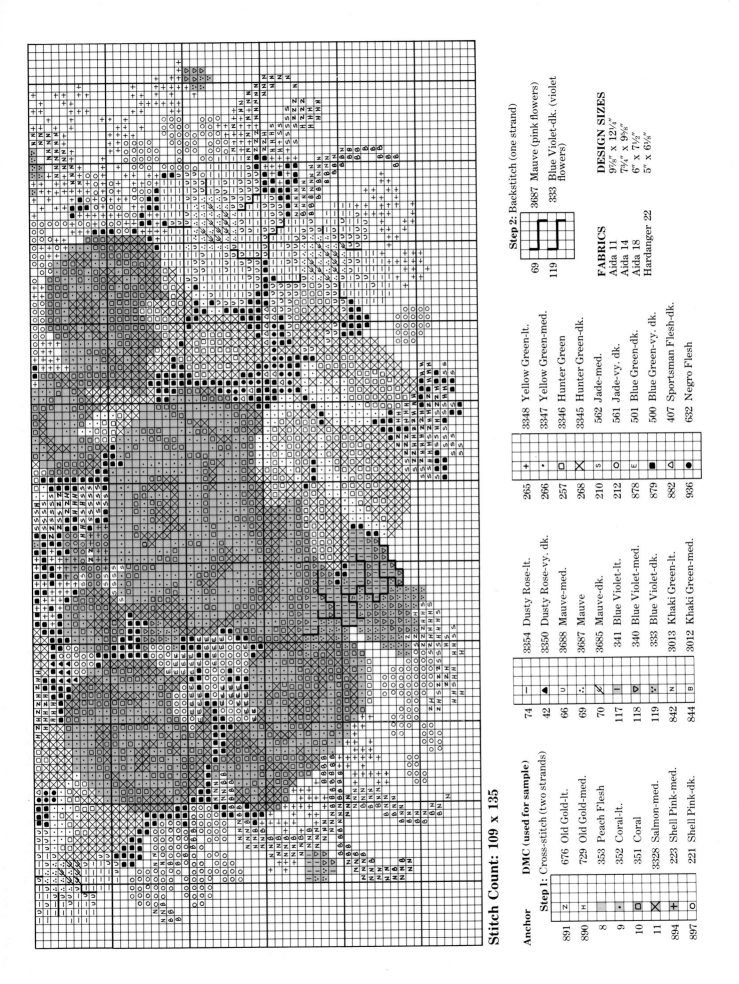

| Anchor | | DMC (used for sample) |
|---|---|---|
| | **Step 1: Cross-stitch (two strands)** | |
| 891 | Z | 676 Old Gold-lt. |
| 890 | H | 729 Old Gold-med. |
| 8 | ▒ | 353 Peach Flesh |
| 9 | · | 352 Coral-lt. |
| 10 | ▢ | 351 Coral |
| 11 | X | 3328 Salmon-med. |
| 894 | + | 223 Shell Pink-med. |
| 897 | O | 221 Shell Pink-dk. |

| 74 | I | 3354 Dusty Rose-lt. |
| 42 | ◀ | 3350 Dusty Rose-vy. dk. |
| 66 | ⊍ | 3688 Mauve-med. |
| 69 | ∴ | 3687 Mauve |
| 70 | ◿ | 3685 Mauve-dk. |
| 117 | ▯ | 341 Blue Violet-lt. |
| 118 | ▷ | 340 Blue Violet-med. |
| 119 | ∴ | 333 Blue Violet-dk. |
| 842 | N | 3013 Khaki Green-lt. |
| 844 | B | 3012 Khaki Green-med. |

| 265 | + | 3348 Yellow Green-lt. |
| 266 | · | 3347 Yellow Green-med. |
| 257 | ▢ | 3346 Hunter Green |
| 268 | X | 3345 Hunter Green-dk. |
| 210 | S | 562 Jade-med. |
| 212 | O | 561 Jade-vy. dk. |
| 878 | E | 501 Blue Green-dk. |
| 879 | ◤ | 500 Blue Green-vy. dk. |
| 882 | ◢ | 407 Sportsman Flesh-dk. |
| 936 | ● | 632 Negro Flesh |

**Step 2: Backstitch (one strand)**

| 69 | | 3687 Mauve (pink flowers) |
| 119 | | 333 Blue Violet-dk. (violet flowers) |

**DESIGN SIZES**

**FABRICS**
Aida 11    9⅞" x 12¼"
Aida 14    7¾" x 9⅝"
Aida 18    6" x 7½"
Hardanger 22    5" x 6⅛"

**11**

# FEBRUARY 4–12
## *Carrot Festival*

Need a cause for celebration? The town of Holtville, California, knows that a good carrot is all the reason you need. Join in the festivities and stitch up this tote. Fill it with a carafe of carrot juice or another favorite beverage, and it's the perfect present for your "thirsty rabbit."

# *Rabbit Tote*

## SAMPLE
Stitched on white Aida 14, the finished design size is 11¼" x 8½". The fabric was cut 14" x 14".

## MATERIALS
Completed cross-stitch on white Aida 14; matching thread
⅝ yard of 45"-wide yellow fabric for lining; matching thread
⅜ yard of polyester fleece
1 yard of ⅜"-wide green polka-dot grosgrain ribbon

## DIRECTIONS
All seam allowances are ¼".

1. Cut the Aida 12" x 13", with the carrot border 1¾" above the bottom 12" edge. Cut the lining fabric 12" x 21". Cut the fleece 12" x 16¾".

2. With the right sides together, stitch the top 12" edge of the Aida to one 12" edge of the lining. Press the seam open. Pin the fleece to the wrong side of the Aida, allowing 4½" of the fleece to extend over the lining.

3. Fold the unit with right sides together to measure 6" x 33½". Stitch all edges, securing the fleece and leaving a 4" opening in the end of the lining. Trim the fleece from the seam allowances and clip the corners. Turn right side out and slipstitch.

4. Fold the lining inside the Aida bag so that the fold is 4¼" from the Aida/lining seam. To make the casing, stitch on the right side of the bag through three layers, along the seam joining the Aida and lining. Stitch a second row parallel to and ½" above the first. Snip the threads in the side seam between the stitching rows.

5. Attach safety pin to one end of ribbon and thread through casing.

| Anchor | | DMC (used for sample) | |
|---|---|---|---|
| | | **Step 1:** Cross-stitch (two strands) | |
| 293 | ∴ | 727 | Topaz-vy. lt. |
| 11 | I | 351 | Coral |
| 40 | X | 956 | Geranium |
| 86 | o / | 3608 | Plum-vy. lt. |
| 117 | ● | 341 | Blue Violet-lt. |
| 204 | · | 912 | Emerald Green-lt. |
| | | **Step 2:** Backstitch (one strand) | |
| 403 | | 310 | Black |
| | | **Step 3:** French Knots (one strand) | |
| 403 | ● | 310 | Black |

| FABRICS | DESIGN SIZES |
|---|---|
| Aida 11 | 14½" x 10⅞" |
| Aida 18 | 8¾" x 6⅝" |
| Hardanger 22 | 7⅛" x 5⅜" |

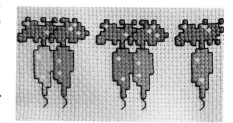

**Stitch Count: 157 x 119**

# FEBRUARY 14
## *Valentine's Day*

One of the numerous stories that surround the origin of Valentine's Day is that the tradition began with the Roman festival of Lupercalia. On that occasion, a young man drew from a box the name of the woman who was to be his sweetheart for the day or the year. This Valentine's Day, draw from our projects and select a dainty piece of cross-stitch to give or to keep.

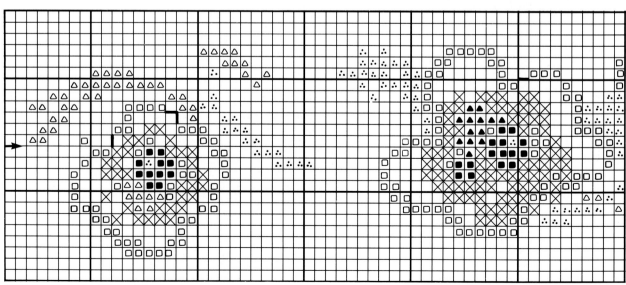

**Stitch Count: 99 x 20**

14

# Flower Garden Towel

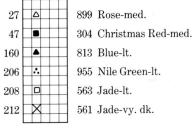

| Anchor | | DMC (used for sample) |
|---|---|---|
| | **Step 1:** Cross-stitch (two strands) | |
| 27 | △ | 899 Rose-med. |
| 47 | ■ | 304 Christmas Red-med. |
| 160 | ▲ | 813 Blue-lt. |
| 206 | ∴ | 955 Nile Green-lt. |
| 208 | □ | 563 Jade-lt. |
| 212 | ✕ | 561 Jade-vy. dk. |
| | **Step 2:** Backstitch (one strand) | |
| 208 | ⌐ | 563 Jade-lt. |

## SAMPLE

Stitched on ivory Jobelan 28 over two threads, the finished design size for one motif is 7⅛" x 1⅜". Cut the Jobelan 20" x 6". Begin stitching the first motif at least 2½" from the left end of the fabric, centering the design vertically. The placement for additional motifs is marked on the graph.

| FABRICS | DESIGN SIZES |
|---|---|
| Aida 11 | 9" x 1⅛" |
| Aida 14 | 7⅛" x 1⅜" |
| Aida 18 | 5½" x 1⅛" |
| Hardanger 22 | 4½" x ⅞" |

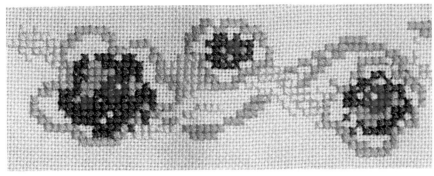

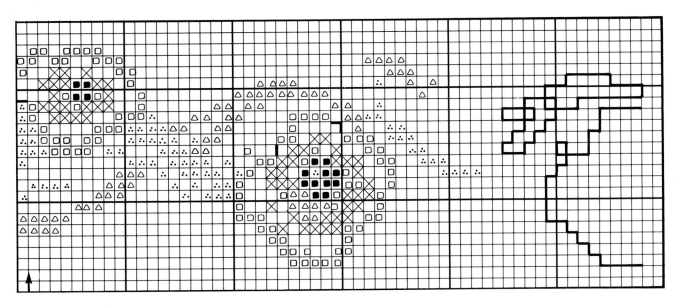

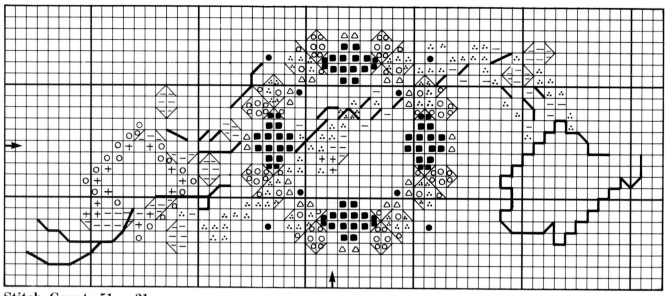

**Stitch Count: 51 x 21**

# Wreath Garland Towel

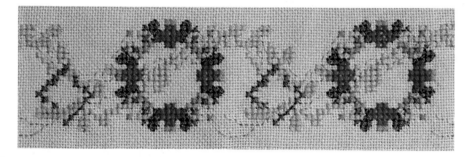

## SAMPLE

Stitched on ivory Jobelan 28 over two threads, the finished design size for one motif is 3⅝" x 1½". Cut the fabric 20" x 6". Begin stitching the first motif at least 2½" from the left side of the fabric, centering the design vertically. Stitch the additional motifs as shown on the graph.

## MATERIALS

Completed cross-stitch on ivory Jobelan 28; matching thread
Unstitched ivory Jobelan for towel, 16" x 26"
½-yard lengths of purchased trims or crocheted borders
½ yard of ½"-wide cream lace trim

## DIRECTIONS

**1.** Cut the stitched piece so that the length is 16" and the design is centered. Cut the width so that the unstitched fabric extends ½" above and ½" below the stitched design.

**2.** Fold under ¼" twice at the ends of the towel; hem by hand. Position the crocheted trims where desired (see the photo). Slipstitch the trim to the towel.

**3.** Fold under ¼" on each long edge of the stitched design piece. Slipstitch both edges to the towel, with the lower edge meeting the edge of the crocheted trim.

**4.** Slipstitch the ½"-wide trim over the top folded edge of the design piece.

**5.** Fold the side edges of the towel ¼" double to the back of the towel; hem by hand, securing the ends of the stitched piece and any raw ends of the trim.

| Anchor | | | DMC (used for sample) |
|--------|---|---|------------------------|
| **Step 1:** | | | Cross-stitch (two strands) |
| 27 | △ | | 899 Rose-med. |
| 47 | ■ | ◢ | 304 Christmas Red-med. |
| 108 | + | | 211 Lavender-lt. |
| 158 | – | ◹ | 828 Blue-ultra vy. lt. |
| 120 | ● | | 794 Cornflower Blue-lt. |
| 206 | ∴ | ◿ | 955 Nile Green-lt. |
| 210 | ○ | ◺ | 562 Jade-med. |

| | | DMC |
|---|---|-----|
| **Step 2:** | | Backstitch (one strand) |
| 158 | 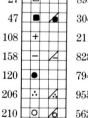 | 828 Blue-ultra vy. lt. |

| FABRICS | DESIGN SIZES |
|---------|--------------|
| Aida 11 | 4⅝" x 1⅞" |
| Aida 14 | 3⅝" x 1½" |
| Aida 18 | 2⅞" x 1⅛" |
| Hardanger 22 | 2⅜" x 1" |

# Valentine
# Boxes

## SAMPLES

Stitched on pink or gray Glenshee Linen 29 over two threads, the finished design size of the largest letter is 1¾" x 1⅜". The fabric was cut 6" x 6".

## MATERIALS (for one box)

Completed cross-stitch on pink or gray Glenshee Linen 29
One 2½" square lace doily
One 3" round box
Acrylic paint; pink or lavender
15" of 1/16"-wide blue rayon braid for pink box; 4" of ⅛"-wide lavender satin ribbon and 11" of ⅛"-wide pink satin ribbon for lavender box
Four ¼"-wide flat gold heart beads
One small piece of fleece
One small piece of lightweight cardboard
Glue

## DIRECTIONS

**1.** Make patterns for a 4" circle and a 2¼" circle. Cut a 4" circle from the linen, with the stitched design centered.

**2.** Cut one 2¼" circle from the cardboard and two from the fleece. Trim ¼" from the edge of one fleece circle.

**3.** Glue the two fleece circles to the cardboard, with the smaller circle on top. Center the design over the fleece and glue in place, keeping the surface taut. Fold the excess fabric to the back. Cut away overlapping fabric so that the layers on the back are flat, and then glue.

**4.** Paint the box. When the paint is dry, center and glue the doily to the lid. Center and glue the design piece over the doily.

**5.** Cut a 4" length of rayon braid for the pink box; fold the remaining braid into two 2" loops. For the lavender box, fold the pink ribbon into 2" loops. For either box, tie the 4" length around the center of the loops. Glue the bow to the box; see the photo for placement. Tie a gold heart bead to each ribbon or braid end. Trim the ends.

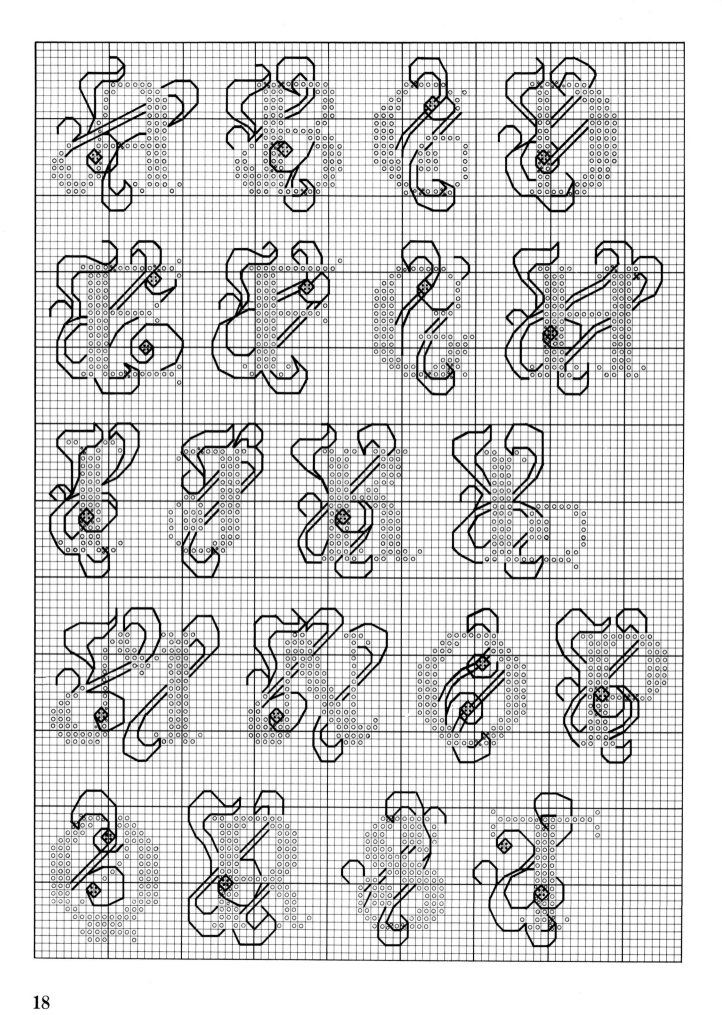

18

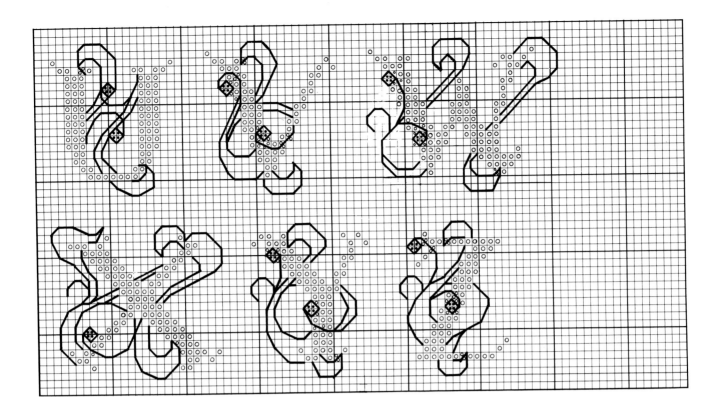

## Pink Box

| Anchor | | DMC (used for sample) |
|---|---|---|
| **Step 1:** Cross-stitch (two strands) | | |
| 969 | o / 6 | 316 Antique Mauve-med. |
| 970 | / ◢ | 315 Antique Mauve-dk. |
| **Step 2:** Backstitch (one strand) | | |
| 970 | ⌐ | 315 Antique Mauve-dk. |

## Lavender Box

| Anchor | | DMC (used for sample) |
|---|---|---|
| **Step 1:** Cross-stitch (two strands) | | |
| 779 | o / 6 | 926 Slate Green-dk. |
| 851 | / ◢ | 924 Slate Green-vy. dk. |
| **Step 2:** Backstitch (one strand) | | |
| 851 | ⌐ | 924 Slate Green-vy. dk. |

| FABRICS | DESIGN SIZES |
|---|---|
| Aida 11 | 2⅜″ x 1⅞″ |
| Aida 14 | 1⅞″ x 1⅜″ |
| Aida 18 | 1½″ x 1⅛″ |
| Hardanger 22 | 1⅛″ x ⅞″ |

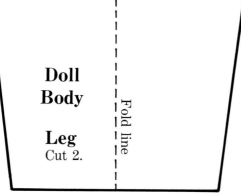

**Doll Body**

**Leg**
Cut 2.

Fold line

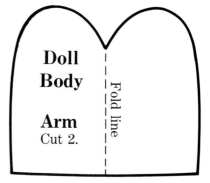

**Doll Body**

**Arm**
Cut 2.

Fold line

# MARCH 3
## Doll Day

In Japan, the Doll Festival is a time for girls to visit and admire each other's doll collections. A typical collection includes 15 dolls, elaborately dressed to resemble the emperor, his wife, and other members of the royal court. Our doll is Emily, and in her beautifully cross-stitched dresses, she'll be a hit at your favorite little girl's royal court.

# Emily

**MATERIALS (for doll's body)**
⅛ yard of white fabric; matching thread
Porcelain parts (see Suppliers)
Stuffing
Glue
Dressmakers' pen
Tracing paper for patterns

**DIRECTIONS**
All seam allowances are ¼".

1. Trace patterns for the doll body front, back, arms, and legs, transferring all information. Trace patterns onto fabric and cut out.

2. Fold arm piece in half, right sides together; stitch along raw edges, leaving the bottom edge open. Turn and stuff. At open end, turn fabric under ¼". Insert a porcelain arm and glue it to fabric. Repeat for second arm. Make the legs in same way but leave both ends open. Turn. At small open end, turn under ¼"; insert a porcelain leg and glue it to fabric; then stuff. Repeat for second leg.

3. Sew darts in the body pieces. With right sides together, sew the body front and back along the side edges. Leave 2" at the top and the entire bottom unstitched. Do not turn.

4. Slide the legs inside the body, aligning the raw edges on the legs with the raw edges on the bottom of the body. Sew across the body and legs. Turn right side out through the top opening. Stuff. Slipstitch the opening closed.

5. Tack the arms to the body and glue the head in place.

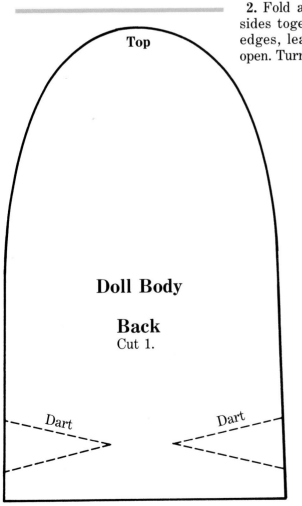

**Doll Body**

**Back**
Cut 1.

Dart    Dart

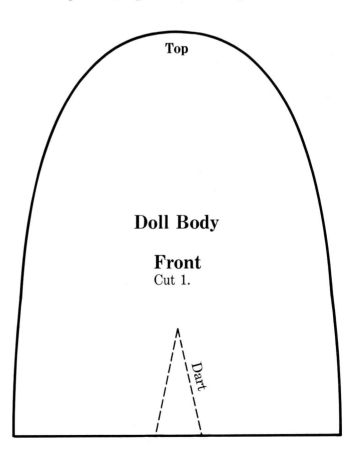

**Doll Body**

**Front**
Cut 1.

Dart

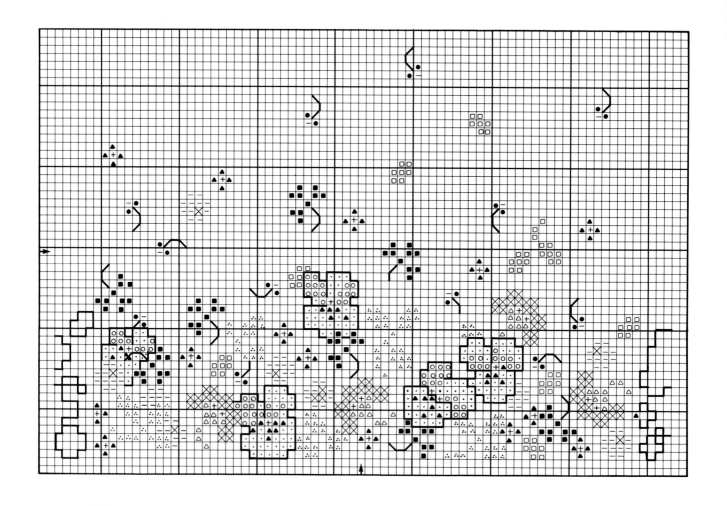

# *Dresses*

## SAMPLES

**Flower-Garden Dress:** Stitched on white fabric, using Waste Canvas 16, the finished skirt design is 3¼″ high. Cut the fabric for the skirt 23″ x 7″; cut the waste canvas 23″ x 4½″. Begin stitching in the center of the skirt, 1½″ from the lower long edge, and repeat the design all the way around the skirt. Lines on the graph show the placement of repeats.

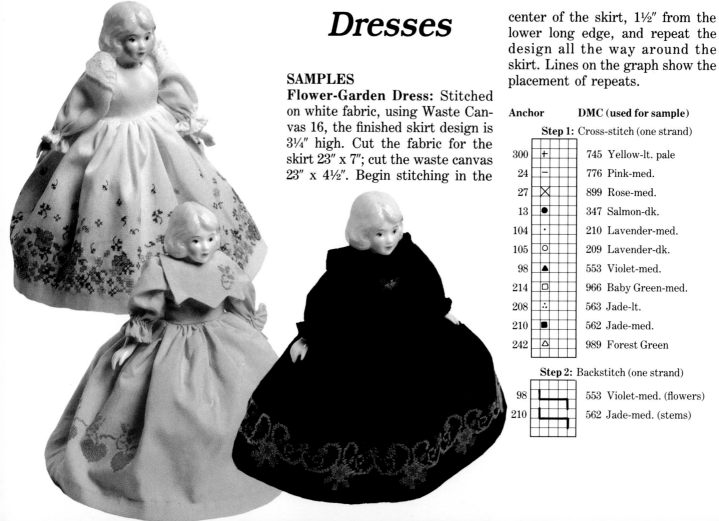

| Anchor | | DMC (used for sample) |
|---|---|---|
| **Step 1:** Cross-stitch (one strand) | | |
| 300 | + | 745 Yellow-lt. pale |
| 24 | − | 776 Pink-med. |
| 27 | X | 899 Rose-med. |
| 13 | ● | 347 Salmon-dk. |
| 104 | · | 210 Lavender-med. |
| 105 | ○ | 209 Lavender-dk. |
| 98 | ▲ | 553 Violet-med. |
| 214 | □ | 966 Baby Green-med. |
| 208 | ∴ | 563 Jade-lt. |
| 210 | ■ | 562 Jade-med. |
| 242 | △ | 989 Forest Green |

| | | |
|---|---|---|
| **Step 2:** Backstitch (one strand) | | |
| 98 | | 553 Violet-med. (flowers) |
| 210 | | 562 Jade-med. (stems) |

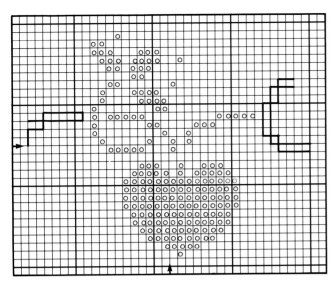

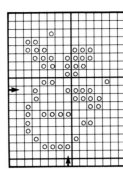

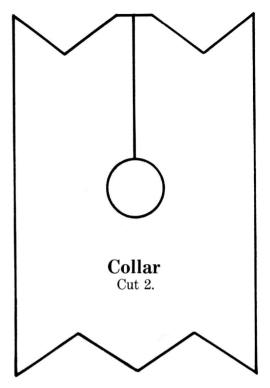

**Pretty Pink Hearts Dress:**
Stitched on pink fabric using
Waste Canvas 20, the finished
skirt design (three repeats of the
motif) is 3⅛" x 1⅜". Cut the fabric
for the skirt 23" x 7"; cut the waste
canvas 5" x 2½". Begin stitching
the center heart 4¼" from the center front of the skirt and 2" from
the lower long edge (see photo).
Repeat the motif on both sides of

the first motif. Lines on the graph
show the placement of repeats. Before stitching the collar, trace the
pattern onto the fabric. Position
the stitching on the collar (see
photo).

| Anchor | | DMC (used for sample) |
|---|---|---|

**Step 1:** Cross-stitch (one strand)

| 66 | o | 3688 Mauve-med. |
|---|---|---|

**Collar**
Cut 2.

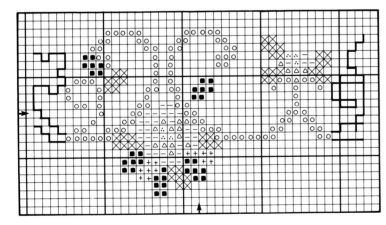

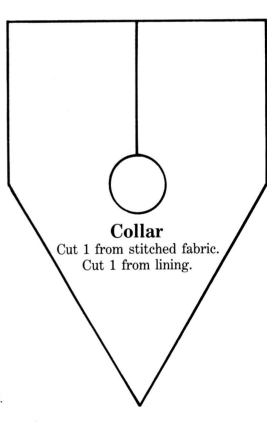

**Winter Holiday Dress:** Stitched
on dark green fabric using Waste
Canvas 16, the finished skirt design is 1¼" high. Cut the fabric for
the skirt 23" x 7"; cut the waste
canvas 23" x 2½". Begin stitching
in the center of the skirt, 1½" from
the lower long edge. Lines on the
graph show the placement of repeats. For the collar, trace the pattern onto the fabric before
stitching. Center and stitch only
the small flower motif on the front

of the collar (see photo).

| Anchor | | DMC (used for sample) |
|---|---|---|

**Step 1:** Cross-stitch (one strand)

| 901 | o | 680 Old Gold-dk. |
|---|---|---|
| 10 | − | 352 Coral-lt. |
| 11 | △ | 3328 Salmon-med. |
| 13 | ∴ | 347 Salmon-dk. |
| 215 | + | 320 Pistachio Green-med. |
| 266 | ■ | 3347 Yellow Green-med. |
| 257 | ✕ | 3346 Hunter Green |

**Collar**
Cut 1 from stitched fabric.
Cut 1 from lining.

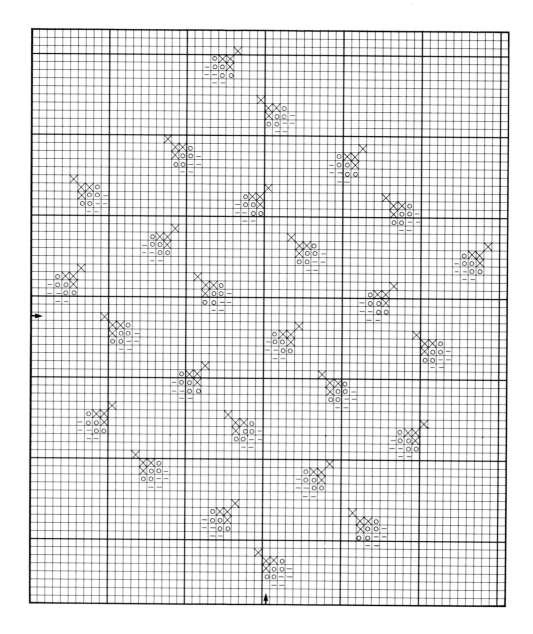

**Scalloped-Collar Dress:** The design was stitched on white Aida 18. Before stitching the collar, trace the pattern onto the fabric. Stitch the entire collar (see photo).

| Anchor | | DMC (used for sample) |
|---|---|---|
| | **Step 1:** Cross-stitch (one strand) | |
| 48 | — | 818 Baby Pink |
| 24 | O | 776 Pink-med. |
| 185 | X | 964 Seagreen-lt. |

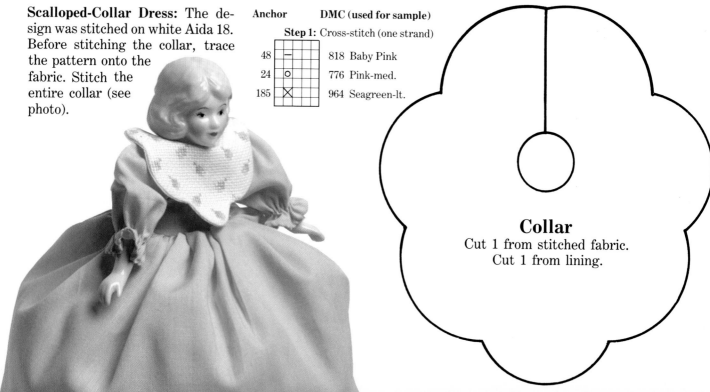

**Collar**
Cut 1 from stitched fabric.
Cut 1 from lining.

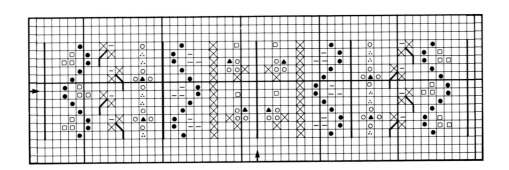

**Satin V-Collar Dress:** Stitched on cream satin fabric using Waste Canvas 20, the finished design is 2¾″ wide. Before stitching, trace the pattern for the collar onto the fabric. Center the design from left to right and repeat to fill the collar from back to front.

| Anchor | | DMC (used for sample) |
|---|---|---|

**Step 1:** Cross-stitch (one strand)

| | | | |
|---|---|---|---|
| 969 | − | 316 | Antique Mauve-med. |
| 869 | o | 3042 | Antique Violet-lt. |
| 871 | ▲ | 3041 | Antique Violet-med. |
| 920 | ◻ | 932 | Antique Blue-lt. |
| 875 | ✕ | 503 | Blue Green-med. |
| 876 | ∴ | 502 | Blue Green |
| 878 | ● | 501 | Blue Green-dk. |

**Step 2:** Backstitch (one strand)

| | | | |
|---|---|---|---|
| 875 | | 503 | Blue Green-med. |

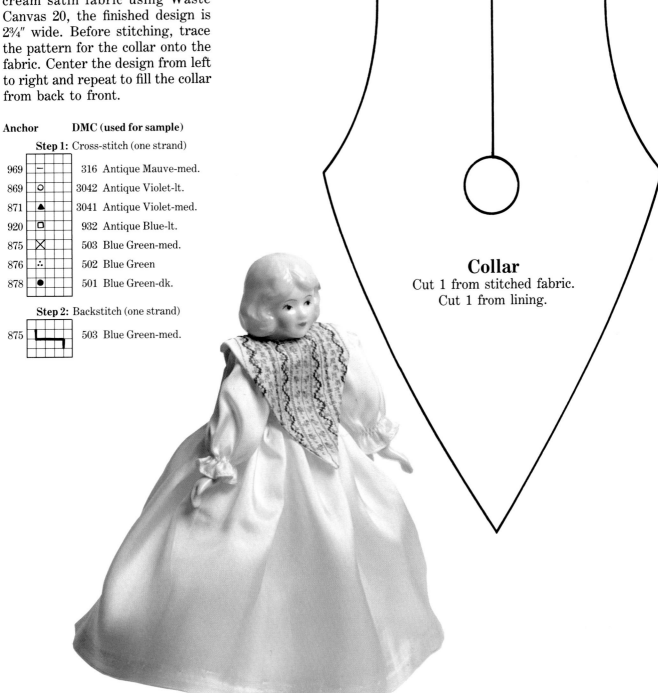

**Collar**
Cut 1 from stitched fabric.
Cut 1 from lining.

**MATERIALS (for one dress)**
¼ yard of 45″-wide fabric; matching thread (see sample information for individual dresses)
Optional: four small snaps
Optional: elastic thread
Tracing paper for patterns
Dressmakers' pen
Flower-Garden Dress: 12″ of 1½″-wide white lace
Satin Dress: 18″ of ¼″-wide dark green picot ribbon

**DIRECTIONS**
All seam allowances are ⅛″.

1. Trace and cut out patterns for all dress pieces. Before cutting any of the dress pieces, see the sample information for the stitched design. For a skirt without cross-stitch, cut the fabric 22″ x 6½″. For the Flower-Garden and Winter Holiday dresses, trim the stitched skirt to 22″ x 6½″ with the design 1½″ from the lower long edge. For the Pretty Pink Hearts dress, trim the skirt to 22″ x 6½″ with the design 1¾″ from the lower long edge. Cut the remaining pattern pieces for the collar, bodice front, bodice back, and sleeve, transferring all information.

2. With the right sides of one bodice front and two bodice back pieces together, stitch the shoulders. Repeat for the remaining bodice front and bodice back pieces for lining.

3. With the right sides of the two bodices together and the shoulder seams matching, stitch up one center back, around the neck, and down the second center back. Clip the curved edges. Turn right side out. As you continue, handle both layers of the bodice as one.

4. Stitch a narrow hem in the wrist edge of each sleeve.

5. For the Flower-Garden dress, cut the lace in half. Baste the lace across the sleeve cap with the edge of the lace parallel to the wrist (see photo).

6. Stitch two rows of gathering threads in one sleeve cap. Gather the sleeve to fit the armhole. With right sides together, stitch the sleeve cap to the bodice. Repeat for the remaining sleeve cap.

7. With the right sides of the bodice and sleeve together, stitch one side seam. Repeat for the remaining side. By hand, sew elastic thread ¼″ above the hem at the wrist. Gather to fit the doll and secure. Option: If doll is to be for display only, sew gathers with regular thread and secure, making an exact fit.

8. Fold the skirt with right sides together. For the back center seam, stitch the short ends together to within 2″ of the top edge; backstitch. Fold the edges of the 2″ opening double to the wrong side and stitch a narrow hem.

9. Mark the center front of the top edge of the skirt. Stitch gathering threads along the top edge. Along the lower edge of the skirt, fold ½″ of fabric double to the wrong side and hem.

10. Mark the center front of the bodice at the waist. Gather the skirt to fit the bodice. Match the center of the skirt to the center of the bodice and stitch. Sew snaps on the center back opening of the dress at the neck and the waist. Option: If doll is for display only, omit snaps and slipstitch opening closed.

11. Place the two collar pieces right sides together. Stitch the outside edges and center back seams. Clip the corners and inside points; turn right side out. Fold ⅛″ of the edges around the neck to the inside; slipstitch.

12. Sew snaps to the top and bottom of the center back opening of the collar. V-Collar Dress: tie the ribbon around the waist, making a bow at the back.

# Pantalets

**MATERIALS (for one pair)**
¼ yard of 45″-wide lightweight fabric; matching thread
12″ of ⅛″-wide elastic
Elastic thread
Tracing paper for pattern
Dressmakers' pen

**DIRECTIONS**
All seam allowances are ⅛″.

1. Trace and cut out the pattern for the pantalets. Cut out the pieces from fabric.

2. With right sides together, stitch the center front and center back seams. Then stitch inseams.

3. Fold ½″ to the wrong side at the waist. To make a casing, turn under the raw edge and stitch, leaving an opening. Cut a 6″ length of elastic and thread through the casing. Overlap the ends ½″ and secure. Slipstitch the casing closed.

4. Stitch a narrow hem in each leg. By hand, sew elastic thread ½″ above the hem. Gather to fit the doll and secure.

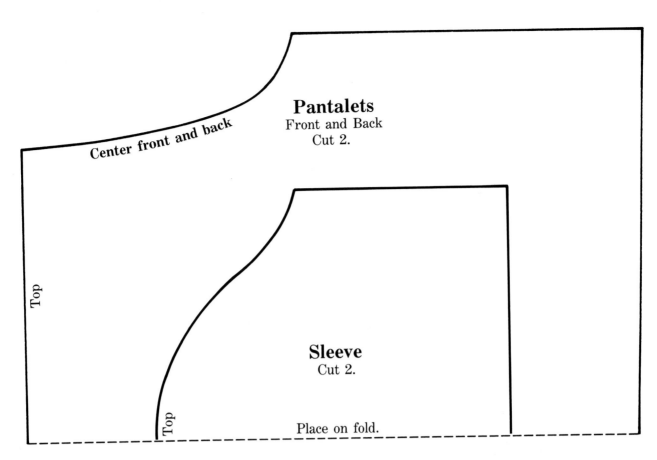

**Pantalets**
Front and Back
Cut 2.

Center front and back

Top

**Sleeve**
Cut 2.

Top

Place on fold.

# *Petticoat*

**MATERIALS (for one)**
½ yard of 6″-wide eyelet or one
  18″ x 6″ piece of fabric to match
  dress
4″ length of ⅛″-wide elastic

**DIRECTIONS**

1. Fold the eyelet or fabric with
right sides together and stitch the
6″ ends.

2. If using plain fabric, stitch a
narrow hem in one long edge.
(Eyelet will not need a hem.)

3. On the opposite long edge,
make a casing by folding ¼″ double
to the wrong side and stitching
close to the bottom fold. Leave an
opening. Insert the elastic and
stitch to secure the ends. Stitch
the opening closed.

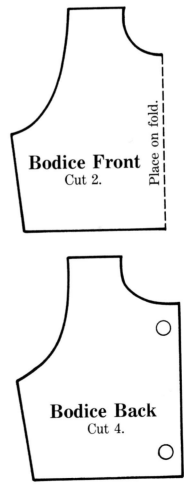

**Bodice Front**
Cut 2.

Place on fold.

**Bodice Back**
Cut 4.

# National Wildlife Week

Animals have provided man with food, clothing, implements, and ornaments since ancient times. Celebrate the beauty of these forest friends with a cross-stitched banner.

# Wildlife Banner

## SAMPLES
Designs are stitched on Country Cloth 11. Fabric was cut 8" x 8".

## MATERIALS
Four completed cross-stitch designs on Country Cloth 11; matching thread
½ yard of 54"-wide dark brown wool fabric; matching thread
⅜ yard of 54"-wide brown/beige pinstripe wool fabric
⅜ yard of 45"-wide stiff sew-in interfacing
2½ yards of small cording

## DIRECTIONS
All seam allowances are ¼".

**1.** Cut each piece of the Country Cloth 6" square, with the design centered.

**2.** Cut one 32½" x 10" piece of dark brown wool for the back of the banner. Cut two 2½" x 28½" pieces for the sides, two 2½" x 10" pieces for the ends, three 2½" x 6" pieces for the center, and two 2½" x 5" pieces for the tabs.

**3.** Cut two 2½" x 40" strips from pinstripe wool for ties. (Cut the strips on the bias if diagonal stripes are desired for finished ties; see photo.) Cut a 1¼"-wide bias, piecing as needed, to equal 2½ yards. Cover 2½ yards of cording with the bias.

**4.** Cut the interfacing 32½" x 10".

**5.** Place the four design pieces in desired order. With right sides together, stitch three center strips between the designs (Diagram A). Stitch the side strips to this center section; then attach the end strips (Diagram B).

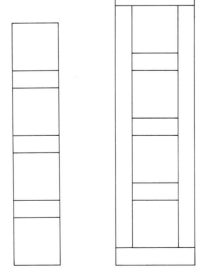

**Diagram A**    **Diagram B**

**6.** Pin the interfacing to the wrong side of the pieced front. With the raw edges aligned, stitch the cording to the right side of the pieced front around the outside edges, rounding the corners slightly.

**7.** Fold one tab piece, with right sides together, to measure 1¼" x 5". Stitch the 5" edge. Turn right side out. Fold the tab in half and pin to the top of the banner front, aligning raw edges (Diagram C). Repeat for the second tab.

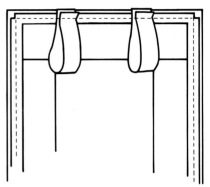

**Diagram C**

**8.** Place the wool backing and the banner front right sides together. Join, sewing on the stitching line for the cording. Leave an opening on one side for turning. Trim the corners and turn right side out. Slipstitch the opening closed.

**9.** Machine-quilt around each design through all layers. Stitch as close as possible to the seam.

**10.** Fold one pinstripe wool strip in half, right sides together, to measure 1¼" x 40". Stitch the long edge and turn right side out. Repeat for second strip. From each 40" length, cut one 11", one 2½", and two 13" lengths. Slipstitch the ends of the 11" length together. Wrap the 2½" length around the center; slipstitch. Trim the ends of the 13" lengths on the diagonal. Fold the raw edges to the inside; slipstitch. Attach one of these two lengths behind each bow. Tack the bows to the front of the banner (see photo).

**Stitch Count: 51 X 49**

**Rabbits:** The finished design size is 4⅝″ x 4½″.

| Anchor | | DMC (used for sample) |
|---|---|---|
| | | **Step 1:** Cross-stitch (three strands) |
| 891 | U | 676 Old Gold-lt. |
| 969 | · | 316 Antique Mauve-med. |
| 970 | Z | 315 Antique Mauve-dk. |
| 266 | ∴ | 471 Avocado Green-vy. lt. |
| 267 | X | 469 Avocado Green |
| 846 | □ | 3051 Gray Green-dk. |
| 862 | ▲ | 934 Black Avocado Green |
| 308 | N | 976 Golden Brown-med. |
| 309 | △ ◿ | 435 Brown-vy. lt. |
| 371 | ● ◿ | 433 Brown-med. |

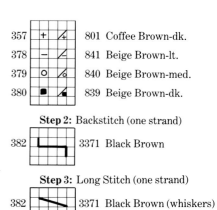

| | | | |
|---|---|---|---|
| 357 | + ◿ | | 801 Coffee Brown-dk. |
| 378 | − ◿ | | 841 Beige Brown-lt. |
| 379 | O ◿ | | 840 Beige Brown-med. |
| 380 | ■ ◥ | | 839 Beige Brown-dk. |

**Step 2:** Backstitch (one strand)

| 382 | | 3371 Black Brown |
|---|---|---|

**Step 3:** Long Stitch (one strand)

| 382 | | 3371 Black Brown (whiskers) |
|---|---|---|

| FABRICS | DESIGN SIZES |
|---|---|
| Aida 11 | 4⅝″ x 4½″ |
| Aida 14 | 3⅝″ x 3½″ |
| Aida 18 | 2⅞″ x 2¾″ |
| Hardanger 22 | 2⅜″ x 2¼″ |

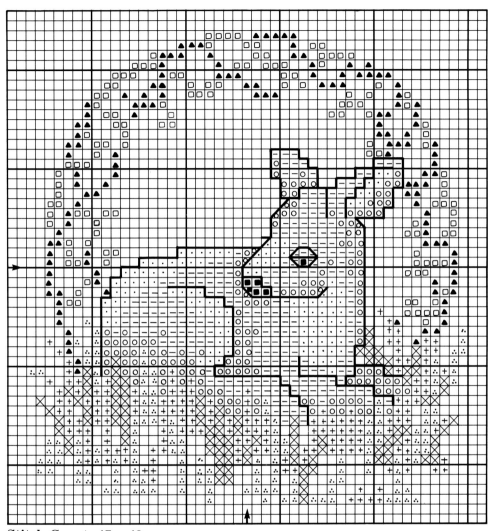

**Stitch Count: 47 x 48**

**Deer:** The finished design size is 4¼″ x 4⅜″.

| Anchor | | DMC (used for sample) |
|---|---|---|
| | | **Step 1:** Cross-stitch (three strands) |
| 266 | ∴ | 471 Avocado Green-vy. lt. |
| 267 | ✕ | 469 Avocado Green |
| 859 | + | 3052 Gray Green-med. |
| 846 | □ | 3051 Gray Green-dk. |
| 862 | ▲ | 934 Black Avocado Green |
| 376 | · ╱ | 842 Beige Brown-vy. lt. |
| 378 | – ╱ | 841 Beige Brown-lt. |
| 379 | o ╱ | 840 Beige Brown-med. |
| 380 | ■ ╱ | 839 Beige Brown-dk. |

**Step 2:** Backstitch (one strand)

| 382 | | 3371 Black Brown |
|---|---|---|

**FABRICS**
Aida 11
Aida 14
Aida 18
Hardanger 22

**DESIGN SIZES**
4¼″ x 4⅜″
3⅜″ x 3⅜″
2⅝″ x 2⅝″
2⅛″ x 2⅛″

**Stitch Count: 47 x 54**

**Squirrels:** The finished design size is 4¼″ x 4⅞″.

| Anchor | | DMC (used for sample) |
|---|---|---|
| | | **Step 1:** Cross-stitch (three strands) |
| 844 | + | 3012 Khaki Green-med. |
| 846 | □ ⟋ | 3051 Gray Green-dk. |
| 862 | ▲ | 934 Black Avocado Green |
| 887 | z | 3046 Yellow Beige-med. |
| 373 | ∴ | 3045 Yellow Beige-dk. |
| 307 | • ⟋ | 783 Christmas Gold |
| 308 | ✕ ⟋ | 782 Topaz-med. |
| 309 | △ ⟋ | 435 Brown-vy. lt. |
| 371 | ● ⟋ | 433 Brown-med. |
| 378 | — ⟋ | 841 Beige Brown-lt. |
| 379 | ○ ⟋ | 840 Beige Brown-med. |
| 380 | ■ ⟋ | 839 Beige Brown-dk. |

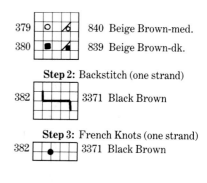

**Step 2:** Backstitch (one strand)

| 382 | ⌐ | 3371 Black Brown |
|---|---|---|

**Step 3:** French Knots (one strand)

| 382 | ● | 3371 Black Brown |
|---|---|---|

| FABRICS | DESIGN SIZES |
|---|---|
| Aida 11 | 4¼″ x 4⅞″ |
| Aida 14 | 3⅜″ x 3⅞″ |
| Aida 18 | 2⅝″ x 3″ |
| Hardanger 22 | 2⅛″ x 2½″ |

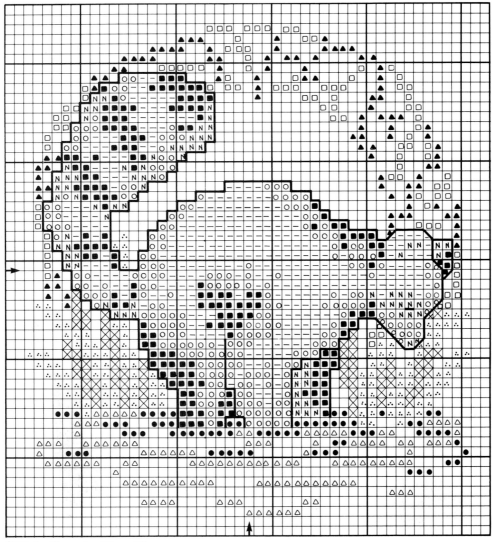

**Stitch Count: 47 x 50**

**Raccoon:** The finished design size is 4¼″ x 4½″.

| Anchor | | DMC (used for sample) |
|---|---|---|

Step 1: Cross-stitch (three strands)

| Anchor | | | DMC (used for sample) |
|---|---|---|---|
| 920 | △ | | 932 Antique Blue-lt. |
| 922 | ● | | 930 Antique Blue-dk. |
| 266 | ∴ | ⟋ | 471 Avocado Green-vy. lt. |
| 267 | ✕ | ⟋ | 469 Avocado Green |
| 846 | ▢ | ⟋ | 3051 Gray Green-dk. |
| 862 | ▲ | ⟋ | 934 Black Avocado Green |
| 378 | — | ⟋ | 841 Beige Brown-lt. |
| 379 | ○ | ⟋ | 840 Beige Brown-med. |
| 380 | ■ | ⟋ | 839 Beige Brown-dk. |
| 381 | N | ⟋ | 838 Beige Brown-vy. dk. |

Step 2: Backstitch (one strand)

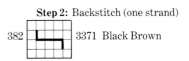

382    3371 Black Brown

| FABRICS | DESIGN SIZES |
|---|---|
| Aida 11 | 4¼″ x 4½″ |
| Aida 14 | 3⅜″ x 3⅝″ |
| Aida 18 | 2⅝″ x 2¾″ |
| Hardanger 22 | 2⅛″ x 2¼″ |

# MARCH 20
## First Day of Spring

The changing colors of the year inspired our Celebration of the Seasons pillow set. Spring's pastel pillow moves us to daydream of fun-filled times to come—picnics in the park, trips to the zoo, hikes in the woods. . . . What's your daydream?

# Spring Pillow

## SAMPLE
Stitched on cream Belfast Linen 32 over two threads, the finished design size is 7″ x 7″. The fabric was cut 17″ x 17″.

## MATERIALS
Completed cross-stitch on cream Belfast Linen 32; matching thread
¾ yard of 45″-wide yellow fabric
2 yards of cream satin double-fold bias tape; matching thread
Dressmakers' pen
14″ knife-edge pillow form

## DIRECTIONS
All seam allowances are ¼″.

1. With the design centered, cut a 13½″ square from the linen.

2. Cut one 13½″ square from yellow fabric for the pillow backing. Also cut four 5″ x 17″ bias strips for ruffles.

3. Draw a line down the lengthwise center of each strip. Place the raw edge of the bias tape next to the line, right sides together, and stitch ¼″ from the edge. Fold the tape back over the line and, keeping the tape smooth, topstitch it to the strip. Repeat with the remaining strips.

4. Fold one strip with right sides together to measure 2½″ wide; stitch the ends. Turn right side out. Press the strip with the fold in the center of the bias tape. Repeat with the three remaining strips.

5. Stitch a gathering thread close to the raw edges of one strip. Gather slightly to 13″; repeat for remaining strips to make four ruffles. Place the ruffles on the pillow top with right sides together, raw edges aligned, and the ends of ruffles ¼″ from the pillow corners. Baste in place.

6. Place the pillow back and top, right sides together, with ruffles tucked between them. Stitch, leaving a 5″ opening for turning. Clip the corners and turn right side out. Insert pillow form. Slipstitch the opening closed.

**Stitch Count: 112 x 112**

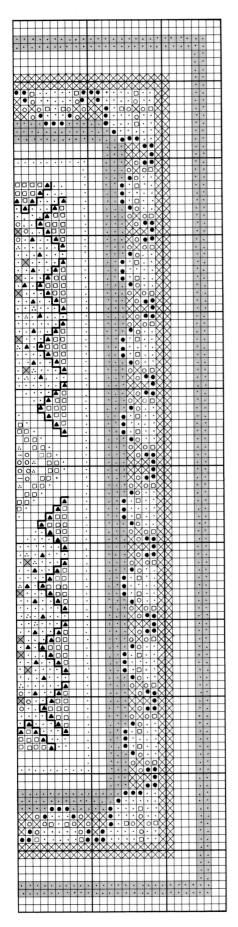

Anchor        DMC (used for sample)

**Step 1:** Cross-stitch (two strands)

| Anchor | Symbol | DMC | Color |
|---|---|---|---|
| 926 | J | | Ecru |
| 292 | · | 3078 | Golden Yellow-vy. lt. |
| 295 | + | 726 | Topaz-lt. |
| 306 | ■ | 725 | Topaz |
| 8 | − | 353 | Peach Flesh |
| 50 | ▽ | 605 | Cranberry-vy. lt. |
| 26 | ✕ | 3708 | Melon-lt. |
| 27 | ✕ | 899 | Rose-med. |
| 42 | U | 3350 | Dusty Rose-vy. dk. |
| 104 | ○ | 210 | Lavender-med. |
| 159 | · | 827 | Blue-vy. lt. |
| 130 | ● | 809 | Delft |
| 206 | □ | 955 | Nile Green-lt. |
| 209 | ▲ | 913 | Nile Green-med. |
| 210 | ∴ | 562 | Jade-med. |
| 379 | ⁚⁚ | 840 | Beige Brown-med. |
| 398 | △ | 415 | Pearl Gray |
| 905 | G | 645 | Beaver Gray-vy. dk. |

**Step 2:** Backstitch (one strand)

| Anchor | | DMC | Color |
|---|---|---|---|
| 209 | | 913 | Nile Green-med. |
| 905 | | 645 | Beaver Gray-vy. dk. |

**Step 3:** French Knots (one strand)

| Anchor | | DMC | Color |
|---|---|---|---|
| 209 | ● | 913 | Nile Green-med. |

| FABRICS | DESIGN SIZES |
|---|---|
| Aida 11 | 10⅛″ x 10⅛″ |
| Aida 14 | 8″ x 8″ |
| Aida 18 | 6¼″ x 6¼″ |
| Hardanger 22 | 5⅛″ x 5⅛″ |

Stitch Count: 34 x 43

Stitch Count: 32 x 39

## MARCH 26
## *Easter*

Once a forbidden fruit during Lent, the egg became an important part of the Easter celebration when the season of fasting ended. Since the Easter bunny continues to make deliveries, eggs are still a happy part of our holiday today.

# Easter Samplers

### SAMPLES
Designs are stitched on white Aida 14. Fabric for all samplers was cut 10″ x 10″. See Suppliers for information on beads and mats.

**Eggscellent:** The finished design size is 2½″ x 3⅛″.

| Anchor | | DMC (used for sample) |
|---|---|---|

**Step 1:** Backstitch (one strand)

| 74 |  | 3354 Dusty Rose-lt. (see photo for placement) |
|---|---|---|
| 161 | | 826 Blue-med. (lettering) |
| 214 | | 368 Pistachio Green-lt. (see photo for placement) |

**Step 2:** French Knots (one strand)

| 161 | ● | 826 Blue-med. |
|---|---|---|

**Step 3:** Beadwork

| | ○ | Iris (MPR 252T) |
|---|---|---|
| | ■ | Emerald (MPR 332) |

| FABRICS | DESIGN SIZES |
|---|---|
| Aida 11 | 3⅛″ x 4″ |
| Aida 18 | 1⅞″ x 2⅜″ |
| Hardanger 22 | 1½″ x 2″ |

**Top Eggsecutive:** The finished design size is 2¼″ x 2⅞″.

| Anchor | | DMC (used for sample) |
|---|---|---|

**Step 1:** Cross-stitch (two strands)

| 301 | − | 744 Yellow-pale |
|---|---|---|
| 160 | ○ ╱ | 813 Blue-lt. |
| 215 | ■ | 320 Pistachio Green-med. |

**Step 2:** Backstitch (one strand)

| 162 | 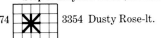 | 825 Blue-dk. |
|---|---|---|

**Step 3:** Smyrna-cross (one strand)

| 74 | ✳ | 3354 Dusty Rose-lt. |
|---|---|---|

| FABRICS | DESIGN SIZES |
|---|---|
| Aida 11 | 3″ x 3½″ |
| Aida 18 | 1¾″ x 2⅛″ |
| Hardanger 22 | 1½″ x 1¾″ |

39

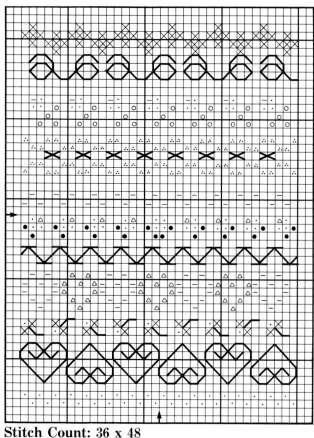

**Stitch Count: 36 x 48**

**Stitch Count: 34 x 44**

## Cross-Stitch Borders: The finished design size is 2⅝″ x 3½″.

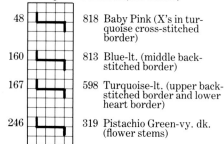

| Anchor | | DMC (used for sample) |
|---|---|---|
| **Step 1:** Cross-stitch (two strands) | | |
| 48 | · | 818 Baby Pink |
| 869 | − | 3042 Antique Violet-lt. |
| 101 | △ | 327 Antique Violet-dk. |
| 160 | X | 813 Blue-lt. |
| 167 | ∴ | 598 Turquoise-lt. |
| 214 | O | 368 Pistachio Green-lt. |
| 246 | ● | 319 Pistachio Green-vy. dk. |

| Anchor | | DMC (used for sample) |
|---|---|---|
| **Step 2:** Backstitch (one strand) | | |
| 48 | | 818 Baby Pink (X's in turquoise cross-stitched border) |
| 160 | | 813 Blue-lt. (middle backstitched border) |
| 167 | | 598 Turquoise-lt. (upper backstitched border and lower heart border) |
| 246 | | 319 Pistachio Green-vy. dk. (flower stems) |

**FABRICS**

| FABRICS | DESIGN SIZES |
|---|---|
| Aida 11 | 3¼″ x 4⅜″ |
| Aida 18 | 2″ x 2⅝″ |
| Hardanger 22 | 1⅝″ x 2⅛″ |

## You're Eggsquisite: The finished design size is 2½″ x 3¼″.

| Anchor | | DMC (used for sample) |
|---|---|---|
| **Step 1:** Backstitch (one strand) | | |
| 101 | | 327 Antique Violet-dk. |

| Anchor | | DMC (used for sample) |
|---|---|---|
| **Step 2:** French Knots (one strand) | | |
| 101 | ● | 327 Antique Violet-dk. |

**Step 3:** Beadwork

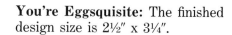

| | | |
|---|---|---|
| ■ | | Old Rose (MPR 553T) |
| △ | | Iris (MPR 252T) |
| X | | Ice Green (MPR 561T) |

| FABRICS | DESIGN SIZES |
|---|---|
| Aida 11 | 3⅛″ x 4″ |
| Aida 14 | 1⅞″ x 2½″ |
| Hardanger 22 | 1½″ x 2″ |

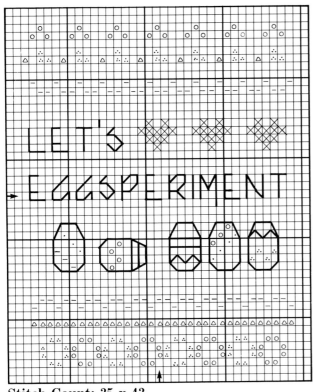

**Stitch Count: 35 x 43**

**Stitch Count: 35 x 39**

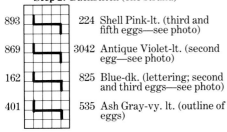

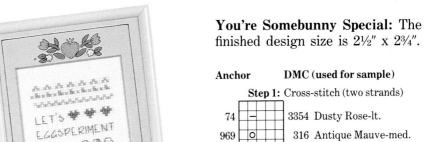

**Let's Eggsperiment:** The finished design size is 2½″ x 3⅛″.

| Anchor | | DMC (used for sample) |
|--------|--|-----------------------|
| | **Step 1: Cross-stitch (two strands)** | |
| 292 | • ╱ | 3078 Golden Yellow-vy. lt. |
| 893 | − | 224 Shell Pink-lt. |
| 969 | ✕ | 316 Antique Mauve-med. |
| 869 | ○ | 3042 Antique Violet-lt. |
| 160 | ∴ | 813 Blue-lt. |
| 214 | △ | 368 Pistachio Green-lt. |

| | | **Step 2: Backstitch (one strand)** |
|---|---|---|
| 893 | | 224 Shell Pink-lt. (third and fifth eggs—see photo) |
| 869 | | 3042 Antique Violet-lt. (second egg—see photo) |
| 162 | | 825 Blue-dk. (lettering; second and third eggs—see photo) |
| 401 | | 535 Ash Gray-vy. lt. (outline of eggs) |

| FABRICS | DESIGN SIZES |
|---------|--------------|
| Aida 11 | 3⅛″ x 4″ |
| Aida 18 | 2″ x 2⅜″ |
| Hardanger 22 | 1⅝″ x 2″ |

**You're Somebunny Special:** The finished design size is 2½″ x 2¾″.

| Anchor | | DMC (used for sample) |
|--------|--|-----------------------|
| | **Step 1: Cross-stitch (two strands)** | |
| 74 | − | 3354 Dusty Rose-lt. |
| 969 | ○ | 316 Antique Mauve-med. |
| 185 | ■ | 964 Seagreen-lt. |
| 214 | ✕ | 368 Pistachio Green-lt. |

| | | **Step 2: Backstitch (one strand)** |
|---|---|---|
| 168 | | 518 Wedgewood-lt. (lettering) |
| 246 | | 319 Pistachio Green-vy. dk. (all else) |

| | | **Step 3: French Knots (one strand)** |
|---|---|---|
| 168 | ● | 518 Wedgewood-lt. |

| | | **Step 4: Beadwork** |
|---|---|---|
| | △ | Lilac (MPR 534) |

| FABRICS | DESIGN SIZES |
|---------|--------------|
| Aida 11 | 3⅛″ x 3½″ |
| Aida 18 | 2″ x 2⅛″ |
| Hardanger 22 | 1⅝″ x 1¾″ |

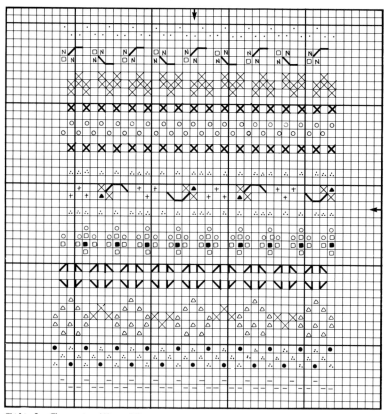

**Stitch Count: 45 x 46**

**Stitch Count: 36 x 44**

**Ribbons and Beads:** The finished design size is 3¼" x 3⅜".

| Anchor | | DMC (used for sample) |
|---|---|---|
| | | **Step 1:** Cross-stitch (two strands) |
| 292 | · | 3078 Golden Yellow.-vy. lt. |
| 48 | − | 818 Baby Pink |
| 893 | △ | 224 Shell Pink-lt. |
| 969 | ✕ | 316 Antique Mauve-med. |
| 70 | ▲ | 3685 Mauve-dk. |
| 167 | ∴ | 598 Turquoise-lt. |
| 214 | ○ | 368 Pistachio Green-lt. |
| 246 | ● | 319 Pistachio Green-vy. dk. |

**Step 2:** Backstitch (one strand)

| 214 | | 368 Pistachio Green-lt. (stems on beaded flowers) |
|---|---|---|
| 246 | | 319 Pistachio Green-vy. dk. (stems on mauve flowers) |

**Step 3:** Beadwork

| + | Pale Peach (MPR 148T) |
|---|---|
| ▢ | Pink (MPR 145T) |
| ◼ | Old Rose (MPR 553T) |
| N | Robin's Egg Blue (MPR 143T) |

**Step 4:** Ribbonwork (1/16"-wide satin)

| ╱ | Yellow couched with one strand of DMC 224 floss |
|---|---|
| ✕ | Pink couched with one strand of DMC 224 floss |

**FABRICS**
Aida 11
Aida 18
Hardanger 22

**DESIGN SIZES**
4⅛" x 4⅛"
2½" x 2½"
2" x 2⅛"

**I'm Eggstremely Fond of You:** The finished design size is 2⅝" x 3¼".

| Anchor | | DMC (used for sample) |
|---|---|---|
| | | **Step 1:** Cross-stitch (two strands) |
| 969 | ✕ | 316 Antique Mauve-med. |

**Step 2:** Backstitch (one strand)

| 161 | | 826 Blue-med. |
|---|---|---|

**Step 3:** Beadwork

| ● | Ice Green (MPR 561T) |
|---|---|

**FABRICS**
Aida 11
Aida 18
Hardanger 22

**DESIGN SIZES**
3¼" x 4"
2" x 2½"
1⅝" x 2"

42

**Stitch Count: 34 x 46**

**Somebunny Loves You:** The finished design size is 2½″ x 3⅜″.

| Anchor | | | DMC | (used for sample) |
|---|---|---|---|---|
| **Step 1:** Cross-stitch (two strands) | | | | |
| 292 | · | | 3078 | Yellow-vy. lt. |
| 48 | − | | 818 | Baby Pink |
| 893 | ● | | 224 | Shell Pink-lt. |
| 74 | △ | ◿ | 3354 | Dusty Rose-lt. |
| 969 | ✕ | ◿ | 316 | Antique Mauve-med. |
| 214 | ○ | | 368 | Pistachio Green-lt. |

| | | | |
|---|---|---|---|
| **Step 2:** Backstitch (one strand) | | | |
| 246 | ⌐ | 319 | Pistachio Green-vy. dk. |

**Step 3:** Beadwork

Old Rose (MPR 553T)

**FABRICS**
Aida 11
Aida 18
Hardanger 22

**DESIGN SIZES**
3⅛″ x 4⅛″
1⅞″ x 2½″
1½″ x 2⅛″

43

## APRIL 22

*Earth Day*

Dedicated to reclaiming pure air and water for our environment, Earth Day was first observed April 22, 1970. Now "Earth Days" are observed by numerous groups on various days, often on the vernal equinox in March.

# *Mother Nature's Sampler*

**SAMPLE**
Stitched on white Linda 27 over two threads, the finished design size is 9″ x 9″. The fabric was cut 15″ x 15″.

Anchor    DMC (used for sample)

**Step 1:** Cross-stitch (two strands)

| Anchor | | DMC (used for sample) |
|---|---|---|
| 300 | | 745 Yellow-lt. pale |
| 414 | | 754 Peach Flesh-lt. |
| 9 | ▲ | 760 Salmon |
| 49 | ▫ | 3689 Mauve-lt. |
| 27 | + | 899 Rose-med. |
| 104 | ○ | 210 Lavender-med. |
| 105 | ● | 209 Lavender-dk. |
| 117 | ✕ | 341 Blue Violet-lt. |
| 214 | · | 966 Baby Green-med. |
| 876 | △ | 502 Blue Green |
| 882 | ◼ | 407 Sportsman Flesh-dk. |

**Step 2:** Backstitch (one strand)

| 905 | | 645 Beaver Gray-vy. dk. |
|---|---|---|

**FABRICS**

**DESIGN SIZES**

| FABRICS | DESIGN SIZES |
|---|---|
| Aida 11 | 11⅛" x 11⅛" |
| Aida 14 | 8¾" x 8¾" |
| Aida 18 | 6¾" x 6¾" |
| Hardanger 22 | 5½" x 5½" |

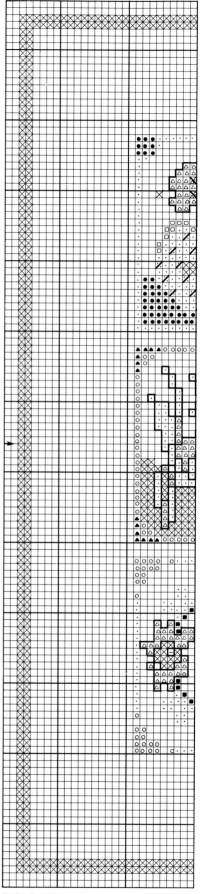

**Stitch Count: 122 x 122**

47

# The 200th Anniversary of Washington's Inauguration

Two hundred years ago, George Washington, at the age of 57, was sworn in as the first President of the United States of America. Washington had hoped to return to private life following the struggle with the British, but after receiving the vote of every elector, he decided it was his duty to accept the presidency. Serving for eight years, he guided the fledgling nation through uncharted waters. We commemorate the heritage of our country with this unabashedly patriotic sampler.

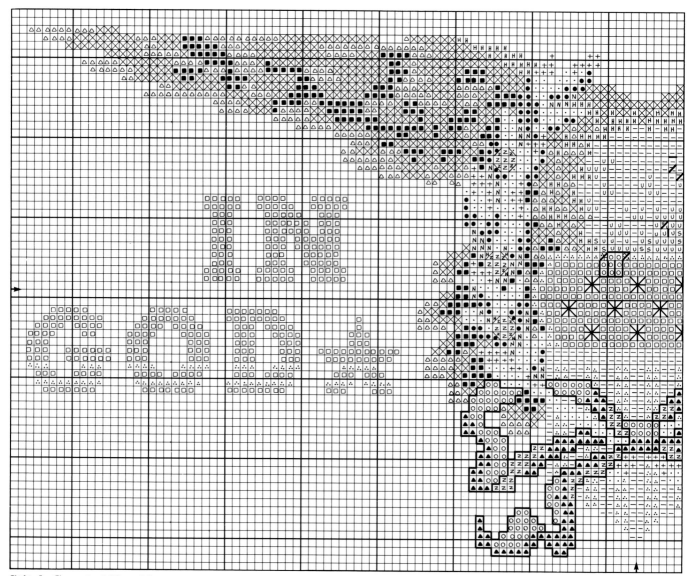

**Stitch Count: 160 x 66**

# In God We Trust

## SAMPLE

Stitched on cream Belfast Linen 32 over two threads, the finished design size is 10″ x 4⅛″. The fabric was cut 16″ x 11″.

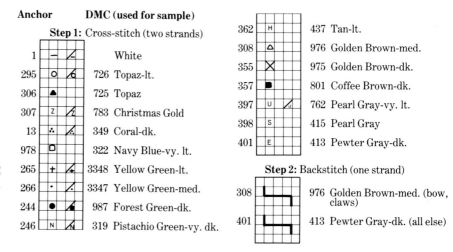

| Anchor | | DMC (used for sample) |
|---|---|---|
| | | **Step 1: Cross-stitch (two strands)** |
| 1 | | White |
| 295 | o | 726 Topaz-lt. |
| 306 | ▲ | 725 Topaz |
| 307 | z | 783 Christmas Gold |
| 13 | ∴ | 349 Coral-dk. |
| 978 | □ | 322 Navy Blue-vy. lt. |
| 265 | + | 3348 Yellow Green-lt. |
| 266 | · | 3347 Yellow Green-med. |
| 244 | ● | 987 Forest Green-dk. |
| 246 | N | 319 Pistachio Green-vy. dk. |
| 362 | H | 437 Tan-lt. |
| 308 | △ | 976 Golden Brown-med. |
| 355 | X | 975 Golden Brown-dk. |
| 357 | ■ | 801 Coffee Brown-dk. |
| 397 | U | 762 Pearl Gray-vy. lt. |
| 398 | S | 415 Pearl Gray |
| 401 | E | 413 Pewter Gray-dk. |

**Step 2: Backstitch (one strand)**

| | | |
|---|---|---|
| 308 | | 976 Golden Brown-med. (bow, claws) |
| 401 | | 413 Pewter Gray-dk. (all else) |

**50**

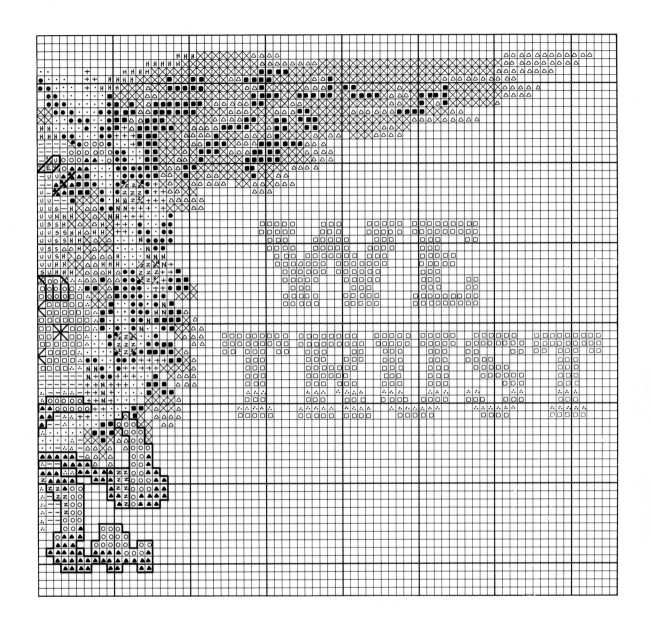

**Step 3:** Smyrna-cross (two strands)

 295    726 Topaz-lt.

**FABRICS**         **DESIGN SIZES**
Aida 11            14½″ x 6″
Aida 14            11⅜″ x 4¾″
Aida 18            8⅞″ x 3⅝″
Hardanger 22       7¼″ x 3″

# Festival of the Hare

The feats and foibles of this leaping, long-eared, long-legged cousin of the cottontail rabbit have been chronicled throughout the centuries. The tale of "The Tortoise and the Hare" has been a favorite of children throughout the world. Today, Turtles International dedicates the official opening of the turtle-racing season to the swiftness of the hare.

## Hare

**SAMPLE**
Stitched on tan Jobelan 28 over two threads, the finished design size is 10⅛" x 4½". The fabric was cut 17" x 11".

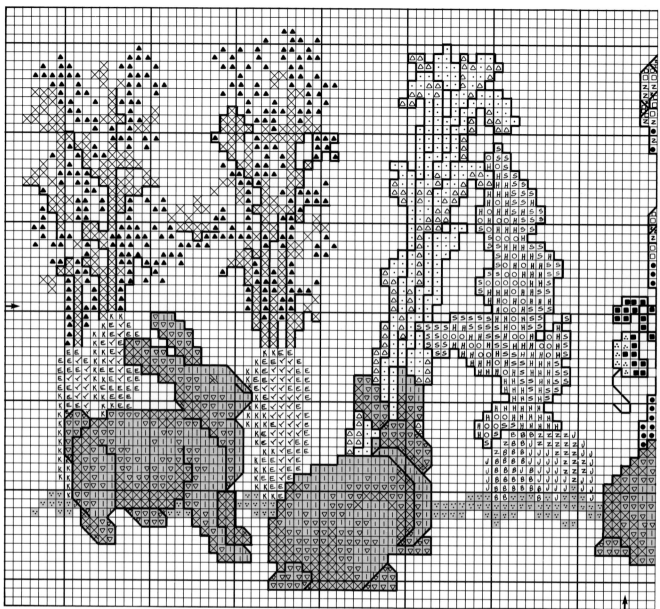

**Stitch Count: 141 x 63**

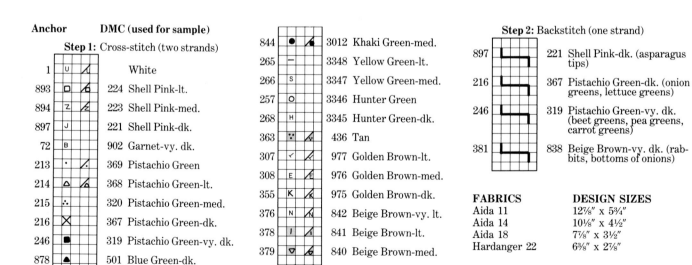

| Anchor | | | DMC (used for sample) |
|---|---|---|---|
| | | | **Step 1: Cross-stitch (two strands)** |
| 1 | U | ◣ | White |
| 893 | ◻ | ◪ | 224 Shell Pink-lt. |
| 894 | Z | ◪ | 223 Shell Pink-med. |
| 897 | J | | 221 Shell Pink-dk. |
| 72 | B | | 902 Garnet-vy. dk. |
| 213 | · | ◪ | 369 Pistachio Green |
| 214 | △ | ◪ | 368 Pistachio Green-lt. |
| 215 | ∴ | | 320 Pistachio Green-med. |
| 216 | ✕ | | 367 Pistachio Green-dk. |
| 246 | ■ | | 319 Pistachio Green-vy. dk. |
| 878 | ▲ | | 501 Blue Green-dk. |
| 842 | + | ◪ | 3013 Khaki Green-lt. |

| | | | |
|---|---|---|---|
| 844 | ● | ◣ | 3012 Khaki Green-med. |
| 265 | — | | 3348 Yellow Green-lt. |
| 266 | S | | 3347 Yellow Green-med. |
| 257 | O | | 3346 Hunter Green |
| 268 | H | | 3345 Hunter Green-dk. |
| 363 | ∴ | ◪ | 436 Tan |
| 307 | ✓ | | 977 Golden Brown-lt. |
| 308 | E | ◪ | 976 Golden Brown-med. |
| 355 | K | ◪ | 975 Golden Brown-dk. |
| 376 | N | ◪ | 842 Beige Brown-vy. lt. |
| 378 | I | ◪ | 841 Beige Brown-lt. |
| 379 | ▽ | ◪ | 840 Beige Brown-med. |
| 380 | ✕ | ◪ | 839 Beige Brown-dk. |

**Step 2: Backstitch (one strand)**

| 897 | | 221 Shell Pink-dk. (asparagus tips) |
|---|---|---|
| 216 | | 367 Pistachio Green-dk. (onion greens, lettuce greens) |
| 246 | | 319 Pistachio Green-vy. dk. (beet greens, pea greens, carrot greens) |
| 381 | | 838 Beige Brown-vy. dk. (rabbits, bottoms of onions) |

**FABRICS**
Aida 11
Aida 14
Aida 18
Hardanger 22

**DESIGN SIZES**
12⅞" x 5¾"
10⅛" x 4½"
7⅞" x 3½"
6⅜" x 2⅞"

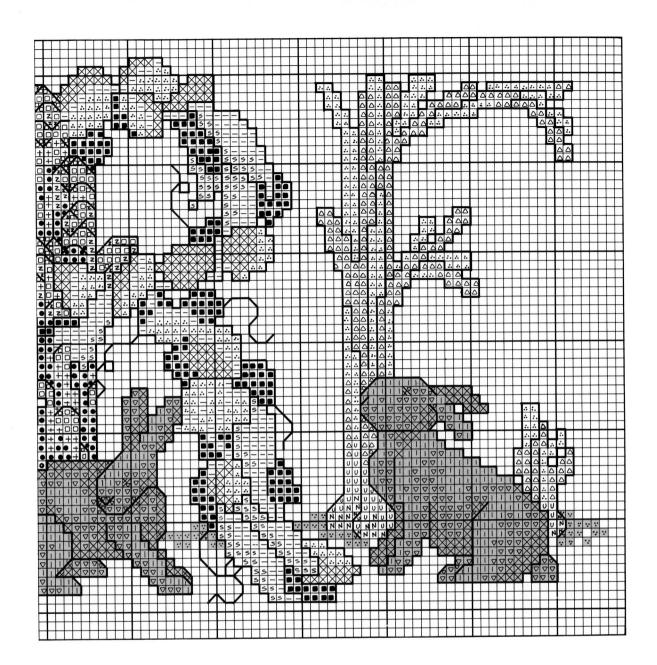

## MAY 6

*The Eiffel Tower's 100th Anniversary*

Vive la France! A trip to France would not be complete without a visit to "la Tour Eiffel," world-renowned landmark of the Paris skyline. Designed and erected by Alexandre Gustave Eiffel to serve as the focal point for the 1889 Universal Exposition in Paris, the 984-foot iron lattice-work tower was at first considered a monstrosity. But today, beloved by all, the Eiffel Tower celebrates its 100th birthday.

# French Countryside

### SAMPLE

Stitched on white Linda 27 over two threads, the finished design size is 13⅞" x 11¾". The fabric was cut 20" x 18".

**Step 1:** Cross-stitch (two strands)

| Anchor | | | DMC (used for sample) |
|---|---|---|---|
| 1 | · | | White |
| 386 | + | | 746 Off White |
| 292 | ⌐ | ◹ | 3078 Golden Yellow-vy. lt. |
| 366 | A | | 951 Sportsman Flesh-vy. lt. |
| 48 | R | ◹ | 818 Baby Pink |
| 24 | J | | 776 Pink-med. |
| 25 | ■ | | 3326 Rose-lt. |
| 74 | M | | 3354 Dusty Rose-lt. |
| 893 | G | | 224 Shell Pink-lt. |
| 894 | ◪ | | 223 Shell Pink-med. |
| 897 | ▲ | ◹ | 221 Shell Pink-dk. |
| 870 | S | | 3042 Antique Violet-lt. |
| 871 | ◩ | | 3041 Antique Violet-med. |
| 101 | ◆ | ◹ | 327 Antique Violet-dk. |
| 159 | ▫ | ◹ | 827 Blue-vy. lt. |

| Anchor | | | DMC (used for sample) |
|---|---|---|---|
| 160 | ◰ | ◹ | 813 Blue-lt. |
| 168 | ▨ | ◹ | 807 Peacock Blue |
| 121 | V | ◹ | 793 Cornflower Blue-med. |
| 940 | ■ | | 792 Cornflower Blue-dk. |
| 213 | I | | 504 Blue Green-lt. |
| 875 | △ | | 503 Blue Green-med. |
| 214 | ▢ | | 368 Pistachio Green-lt. |
| 215 | H | | 320 Pistachio Green-med. |
| 265 | Z | | 3348 Yellow Green-lt. |
| 266 | K | ◹ | 3347 Yellow Green-med. |
| 243 | E | | 988 Forest Green-med. |
| 387 | N | ◹ | 822 Beige Gray-lt. |
| 376 | O | | 842 Beige Brown-vy. lt. |
| 378 | ● | | 841 Beige Brown-lt. |
| 942 | ▬ | ◹ | 738 Tan-vy. lt. |
| 363 | X | ◹ | 436 Tan |
| 309 | ◙ | ◹ | 435 Brown-vy. lt. |
| 347 | ⁙ | ◹ | 402 Mahogany-vy. lt. |
| 308 | ▽ | ◹ | 976 Golden Brown-med. |
| 397 | U | ◿ | 762 Pearl Gray-vy. lt. |
| 398 | ⁖ | ◹ | 415 Pearl Gray |
| 399 | X | | 318 Steel Gray-lt. |
| 400 | W | | 414 Steel Gray-dk. |
| 869 | B | | 453 Shell Gray-lt. |
| 905 | I | ◹ | 645 Beaver Gray-vy. dk. |

**Step 2:** Backstitch (one strand)

| 400 | | 414 Steel Gray-dk. (Eiffel Tower) |
|---|---|---|
| 905 | | 645 Beaver Gray-vy. dk. (all else) |

| FABRICS | DESIGN SIZES |
|---|---|
| Aida 11 | 17⅛" x 14⅜" |
| Aida 14 | 13⅜" x 11¼" |
| Aida 18 | 10½" x 8¾" |
| Hardanger 22 | 8½" x 7⅛" |

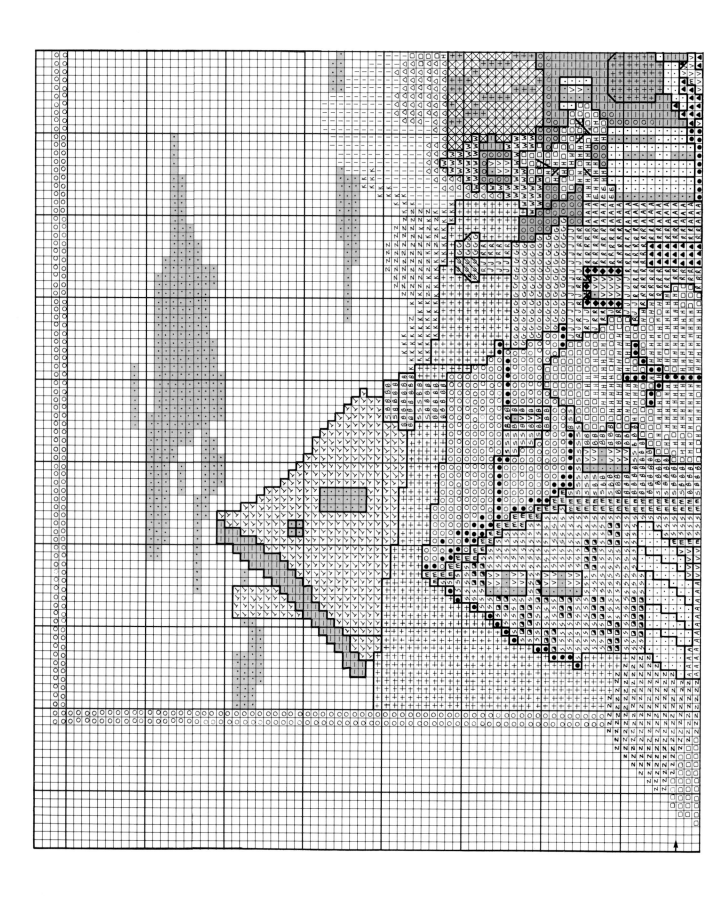

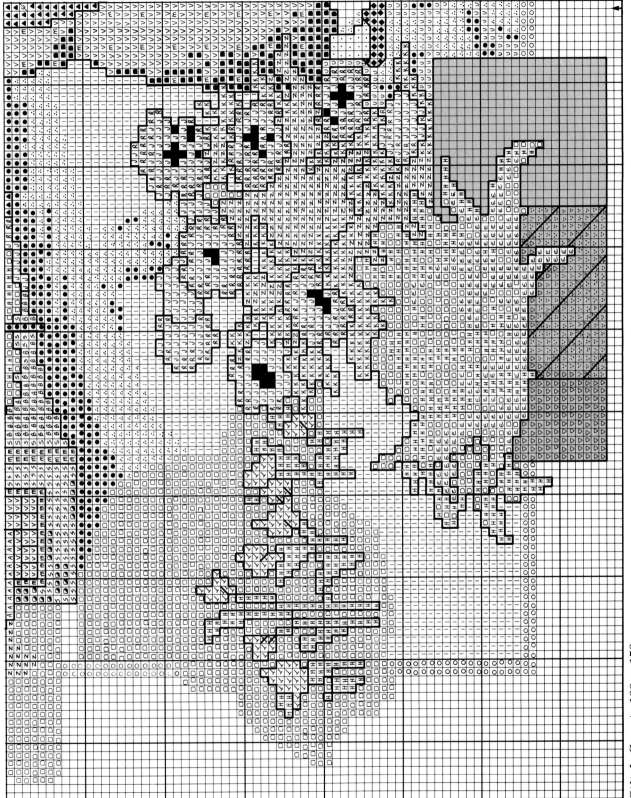

Stitch Count: 188 x 158

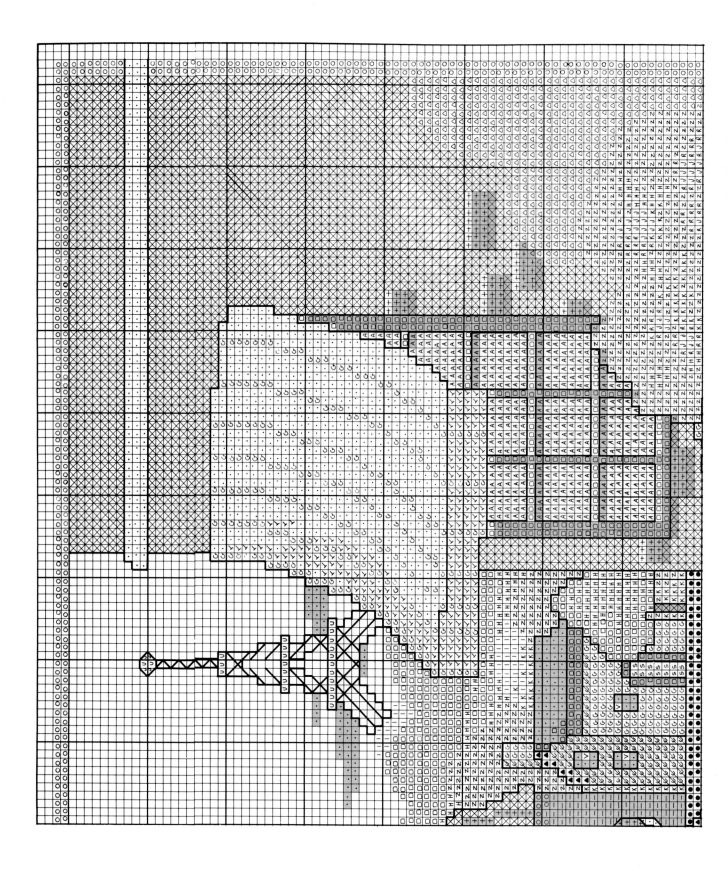

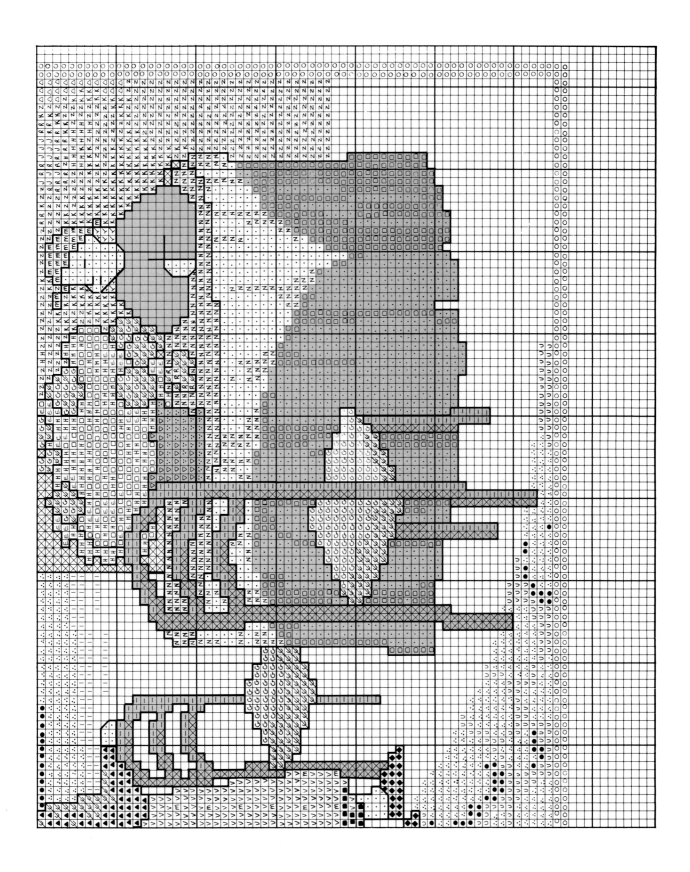

# MAY 14
# *Mother's Day*

It's no wonder that this day is the busiest of the year for telephone companies. Mother's Day fills us with happy thoughts and memories of times together. In addition to giving Mother a call, make the day extra-special with a heartfelt handmade creation.

# *Sachet Pillow*

### SAMPLE
Stitched on cream Belfast Linen 32 over two threads, the finished design size is 3¾" x 4⅛". The fabric was cut 9" x 7". Position design on left half of fabric.

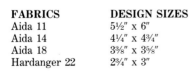

| Anchor | DMC (used for sample) |
|---|---|
| **Step 1:** Backstitch (one strand) | |
| 851 | 924 Slate Green-vy. dk. |
| **Step 2:** French Knots (one strand) | |
| 851 | 924 Slate Green-vy. dk. |

| FABRICS | DESIGN SIZES |
|---|---|
| Aida 11 | 5½" x 6" |
| Aida 14 | 4¼" x 4¾" |
| Aida 18 | 3⅜" x 3⅝" |
| Hardanger 22 | 2¾" x 3" |

**Stitch Count: 60 x 66**

## MATERIALS
Completed cross-stitch on cream
  Belfast Linen 32
One 7″ x 5″ piece of unstitched
  cream Belfast Linen 32 for back
1 yard of 1½″-wide cream flat
  lace; matching thread
1 cup of potpourri

## DIRECTIONS
**1.** Cut the stitched linen 7″ x 5″, with the design centered vertically and 1″ from the left edge.

**2.** With right sides together, stitch the front to the back with a ¼″ seam. Leave a 2″ opening for turning. Clip the corners and turn right side out.

**3.** Fill the sachet with potpourri. Slipstitch the opening closed. Slipstitch the lace to the edges of the sachet, easing in extra fullness at the corners.

# Verb Sampler

## SAMPLE
Stitched on cream Hardanger 22, the finished design size is 8″ x 15¾″. The fabric was cut 14″ x 21″. The center section of the design (the verbs) is to be stitched over one thread; use one strand of floss for this section. Use three strands of floss when stitching over two threads. To accommodate the two sizes of stitches in the sampler, this design must be stitched on a monoweave fabric, such as linen, Linda, or Hardanger.

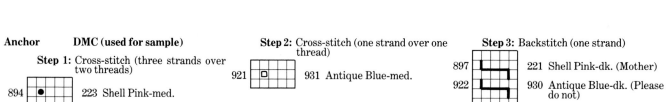

| Anchor | DMC (used for sample) | | Step 2: Cross-stitch (one strand over one thread) | | Step 3: Backstitch (one strand) | |
|---|---|---|---|---|---|---|
| | **Step 1:** Cross-stitch (three strands over two threads) | | 921 □ 931 Antique Blue-med. | | 897 ▬ 221 Shell Pink-dk. (Mother) | |
| 894 | ● | 223 Shell Pink-med. | | | 922 ▬ 930 Antique Blue-dk. (Please do not) | |
| 897 | ✕ | 221 Shell Pink-dk. | | | | |

**64**

**FABRICS**
Dublin Linen 25
Linda 27
Belfast Linen 32

**DESIGN SIZES**
6⅞" x 13¾"
6⅜" x 12¾"
5⅜" x 10¾"

# JUNE
## National Dairy Month

This month, when you drink that refreshing glass of cold milk, take that first scrumptious lick of an ice cream cone, douse your strawberries with sour cream, or spread the butter on corn on the cob, pause for a moment to pay homage to the honorable dairy cow and her wonderful products.

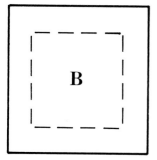

B

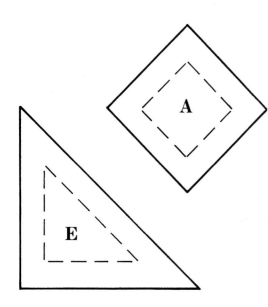

A

E

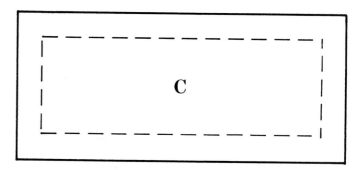

C

D

# Heart Pot Holder

## SAMPLE
Stitched on white Aida 14, the finished design size is 2″ x 2″. The fabric was cut 6″ x 6″.

## MATERIALS
Completed cross-stitch on white Aida 14
¼ yard of 45″-wide blue polished cotton fabric; matching thread
Small pieces of green polished cotton fabric
Small pieces of rose polished cotton fabric; matching thread
Small pieces of white polished cotton fabric
One 7½″ square of polyester fleece
Dressmakers' pen
Material for templates

## DIRECTIONS
All seam allowances are ¼″.

1. Cut a 3½″ square from Aida, with the design centered.

2. Cut one 7½″ square of blue fabric for the backing. For the binding and tab cut a 1⅛″-wide bias strip, piecing as needed, to equal 1 yard.

3. Trace the patterns for the pot holder and cut out. Trace Template A onto rose fabric four times and Template B onto white fabric eight times and green eight times; cut out. Cut out four blue rectangles and four green rectangles using Template C.

4. Stitch the pieces together to form five rows (Diagram A). Then stitch all five rows together to form the block. Fold under the

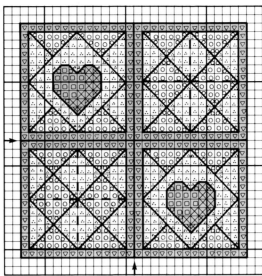

**Stitch Count: 28 x 28**

seam allowance on the diamonds. Topstitch them onto the inner white squares.

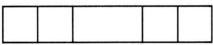
**Row 1**

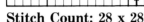
**Row 2**

Aida
**Row 3**

**Row 4**

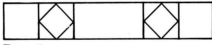
**Row 5**
**Diagram A**

5. Stack the backing right side down; the fleece; and the front, right side up. Baste together. Hand-quilt along all seam lines.

6. Cut a 3″ bias strip for the tab. Stitch the remaining bias strip to the front of the pot holder, right sides together and raw edges aligned. Fold the strip double to the back and slipstitch in place.

7. For a tab, fold under ¼″ on 3″ edges of strip; then fold strip in half lengthwise. Slipstitch folded edges together. Fold tab to measure ¼″ x 1½″. Tuck raw ends under and tack tab securely to back upper left corner.

| Anchor | | DMC (used for sample) | |
|---|---|---|---|
| | **Step 1:** Cross-stitch (two strands) | | |
| 886 | | 677 | Old Gold-vy. lt. |
| 893 | | 224 | Shell Pink-lt. |
| 894 | | 223 | Shell Pink-med. |
| 869 | | 3042 | Antique Violet-lt. |
| 920 | | 932 | Antique Blue-lt. |
| | **Step 2:** Backstitch (one strand) | | |
| 401 | | 844 | Beaver Gray-ultra dk. |

| FABRICS | DESIGN SIZES |
|---|---|
| Aida 11 | 2½″ x 2½″ |
| Aida 18 | 1½″ x 1½″ |
| Hardanger 22 | 1¼″ x 1¼″ |

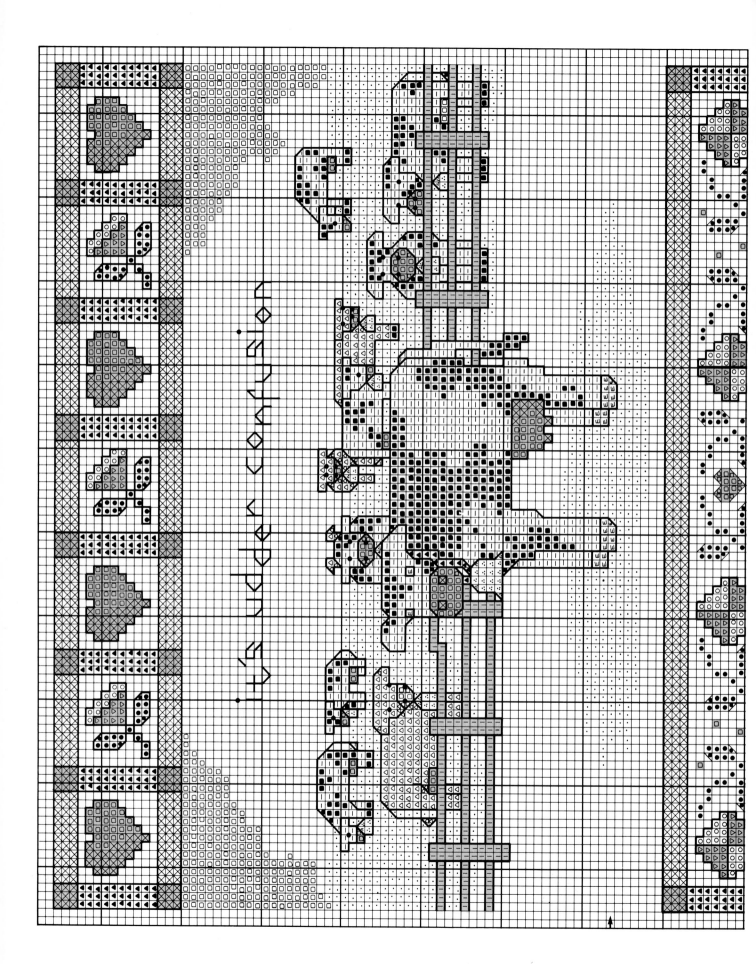

**Stitch Count: 101 x 139**

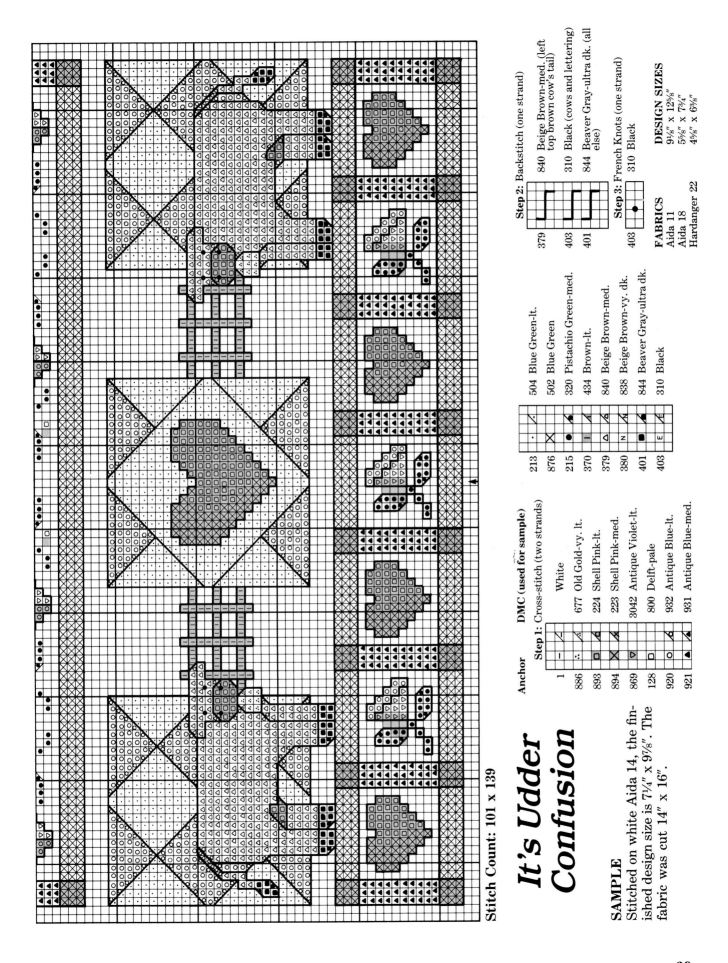

## It's Udder Confusion

**SAMPLE**
Stitched on white Aida 14, the finished design size is 7¼" x 9⅞". The fabric was cut 14" x 16".

| Anchor | | | DMC (used for sample) |
|---|---|---|---|
| **Step 1:** | | | **Cross-stitch (two strands)** |
| 1 | | · | White |
| 886 | - | ∴ | 677 Old Gold-vy. lt. |
| 893 | | ⊡ | 224 Shell Pink-lt. |
| 894 | X | | 223 Shell Pink-med. |
| 869 | | ▷ | 3042 Antique Violet-lt. |
| 128 | □ | | 800 Delft-pale |
| 920 | ○ | | 932 Antique Blue-lt. |
| 921 | ◣ | | 931 Antique Blue-med. |

| | | | |
|---|---|---|---|
| 213 | · | ⩘ | 504 Blue Green-lt. |
| 876 | X | | 502 Blue Green |
| 215 | ● | | 320 Pistachio Green-med. |
| 370 | ◢ | | 434 Brown-lt. |
| 379 | ◪ | | 840 Beige Brown-med. |
| 380 | N | | 838 Beige Brown-vy. dk. |
| 401 | ■ | | 844 Beaver Gray-ultra dk. |
| 403 | E | | 310 Black |

**Step 2:** Backstitch (one strand)

| 379 | | 840 Beige Brown-med. (left top brown cow's tail) |
| 403 | | 310 Black (cows and lettering) |
| 401 | | 844 Beaver Gray-ultra dk. (all else) |

**Step 3:** French Knots (one strand)

| 403 | ● | 310 Black |

**FABRICS**
Aida 11
Aida 18
Hardanger 22

**DESIGN SIZES**
9⅛" x 12⅝"
5⅝" x 7¾"
4⅝" x 6⅜"

**69**

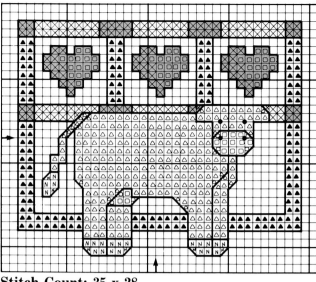

**Stitch Count: 35 x 28**

# Cow Pot Holder

## SAMPLE
Stitched on white Aida 14, the finished design size is 2½″ x 2″. The fabric was cut 6″ x 6″.

## MATERIALS
Completed cross-stitch on white Aida 14
¼ yard of 45″-wide blue polished cotton fabric; matching thread
Small pieces of green polished cotton fabric
Small pieces of rose polished cotton fabric; matching thread
Small pieces of white polished cotton fabric
One 7½″ x 8″ piece of polyester fleece
Dressmakers' pen
Material for templates

## DIRECTIONS
All seam allowances are ¼″.

**1.** Cut the Aida 4″ x 3½″, with the design centered.

**2.** Cut one 7½″ x 8″ piece of blue fabric for the backing. Also cut a 1⅛″-wide bias strip, piecing as needed, to equal 38″.

**3.** Trace patterns B, C, D, and E (page 66) and cut out. Cut out four white, four blue, and four rose squares using Template B. Cut out two green rectangles and two blue rectangles using Template C. Cut two blue rectangles and two green rectangles using Template D. Cut out four white triangles and four blue triangles using Template E.

**4.** Stitch the white triangles to the blue triangles to make four blue-and-white squares.

**5.** Sew the pieces together to form five rows (Diagram B). Then stitch the five rows together to form the block.

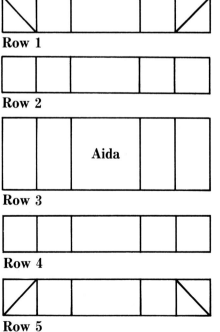

**Row 1**

**Row 2**

**Aida**

**Row 3**

**Row 4**

**Row 5**

**Diagram B**

**6.** Stack the backing right side down; the fleece; and the front, right side up. Baste together. Hand-quilt along all seam lines.

**7.** Cut a 3″ bias strip for the tab. Stitch the remaining bias strip to the front of the pot holder, right sides together and raw edges aligned. Fold the strip double to the back and slipstitch in place.

**8.** For a tab, fold under ¼″ on 3″ edges of strip; then fold strip in half lengthwise. Slipstitch folded edges together. Fold tab to measure ¼″ x 1½″. Tuck raw ends under and tack tab securely to back upper left corner.

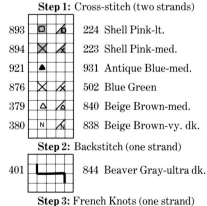

| Anchor | | | DMC (used for sample) | |
|---|---|---|---|---|
| **Step 1:** Cross-stitch (two strands) | | | | |
| 893 | ▫ | ◹ | 224 | Shell Pink-lt. |
| 894 | ✕ | ◹ | 223 | Shell Pink-med. |
| 921 | ▲ | | 931 | Antique Blue-med. |
| 876 | ✕ | ◹ | 502 | Blue Green |
| 379 | △ | ◹ | 840 | Beige Brown-med. |
| 380 | N | ◹ | 838 | Beige Brown-vy. dk. |
| **Step 2:** Backstitch (one strand) | | | | |
| 401 | | | 844 | Beaver Gray-ultra dk. |
| **Step 3:** French Knots (one strand) | | | | |
| 401 | ● | | 844 | Beaver Gray-ultra dk. |

| FABRICS | DESIGN SIZES |
|---|---|
| Aida 11 | 3⅛″ x 2½″ |
| Aida 18 | 2″ x 1½″ |
| Hardanger 22 | 1⅝″ x 1¼″ |

On Dad's special day, let him know just how super he is. Present him with a distinctive sampler created just for him.

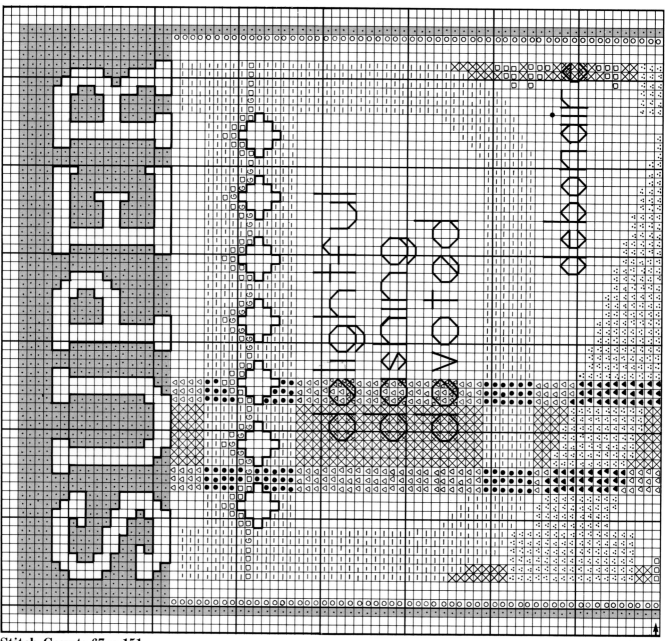

**Stitch Count: 67 x 151**

# *Super Dad*

## SAMPLE

Stitched on oatmeal Floba 25 over two threads, the finished design size is 5⅜″ x 12⅛″. Fabric was cut 12″ x 19″. To personalize the design, transfer the letters to graph paper. Begin stitching the design in the center of the space for the date and name.

| Anchor | | DMC (used for sample) |
|---|---|---|
| **Step 1: Cross-stitch (two strands)** | | |
| 886 | △ | 3047 Yellow Beige-lt. |
| 894 | G | 223 Shell Pink-med. |
| 72 | O | 902 Garnet-vy. dk. |
| 150 | ∴ | 823 Navy Blue-dk. |
| 214 | ▢ | 368 Pistachio Green-lt. |
| 246 | − | 319 Pistachio Green-vy. dk. |
| 876 | • | 502 Blue Green |
| 392 | X | 642 Beige Gray-dk. |

| Anchor | | DMC |
|---|---|---|
| **Step 2: Cross-stitch (blending)** Use two strands–one of each color. | | |
| 886 894 | + | 3047 Yellow Beige-lt. and 223 Shell Pink-med. |
| 886 72 | ■ | 3047 Yellow Beige-lt. and 902 Garnet-vy. dk. |
| 886 150 | ▲ | 3047 Yellow Beige-lt. and 823 Navy Blue-dk. |
| 886 214 | U | 3047 Yellow Beige-lt. and 368 Pistachio Green-lt. |
| 886 246 | ● | 3047 Yellow Beige-lt. and 319 Pistachio Green-vy. dk. |

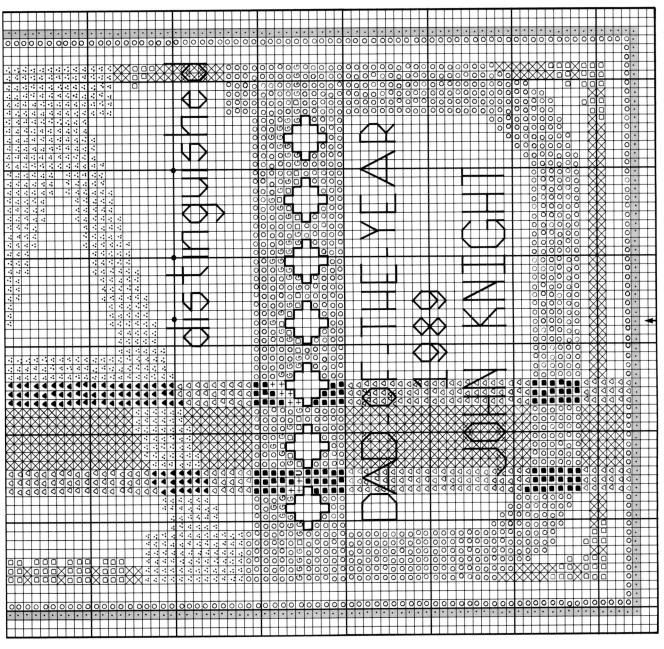

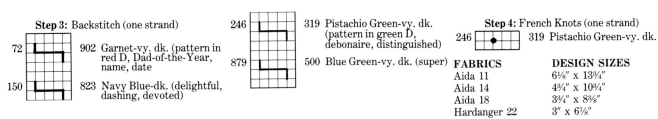

**Step 3: Backstitch (one strand)**

| | | |
|---|---|---|
| 72 | | 902 Garnet-vy. dk. (pattern in red D, Dad-of-the-Year, name, date) |
| 150 | | 823 Navy Blue-dk. (delightful, dashing, devoted) |

| | | |
|---|---|---|
| 246 | | 319 Pistachio Green-vy. dk. (pattern in green D, debonaire, distinguished) |
| 879 | | 500 Blue Green-vy. dk. (super) |

**Step 4: French Knots (one strand)**

| | | |
|---|---|---|
| 246 | ● | 319 Pistachio Green-vy. dk. |

**FABRICS**
Aida 11
Aida 14
Aida 18
Hardanger 22

**DESIGN SIZES**
6⅛" x 13¾"
4¾" x 10¾"
3¾" x 8⅜"
3" x 6⅞"

## JUNE 21

## *First Day of Summer*

What tickles your fancy on sunny summer days? A dip in the pool, a backyard barbecue, a hike on a mountain trail, a cool rush of air on a motorboat ride, an outdoor concert in the park? The bright tints of the season are reflected in the summer pillow for our Celebration of the Seasons pillow set.

# *Summer Pillow*

### SAMPLE
Stitched on cream Belfast Linen 32 over two threads, the finished design size is 7″ x 7″. The fabric was cut 17″ x 17″. See Suppliers for information on ordering beads.

### MATERIALS
Completed cross-stitch on cream Belfast Linen 32; matching thread
¾ yard of 45″-wide light green fabric
2 yards of purchased light blue bias tape; matching thread
Dressmakers' pen
14″ knife-edge pillow form

### DIRECTIONS
All seam allowances are ¼″.

1. With the design centered, cut a 13½″ square from the linen.

2. Cut one 13½″ square from light green fabric for the pillow backing. Also cut four 5″ x 17″ bias strips for ruffles.

3. Draw a line down the lengthwise center of each strip. Place the raw edge of the bias tape next to the line, right sides together, and stitch ¼″ from the edge. Fold the tape back over the line and, keeping the tape smooth, topstitch it to the strip. Repeat with remaining strips.

4. Fold one strip with right sides together to measure 2½″ wide; stitch the ends. Turn right side out. Press the strip with the fold in the center of the bias tape. Repeat with the three remaining strips.

5. Stitch a gathering thread close to the raw edges of one strip. Gather slightly to 13″; repeat for remaining strips to make four ruffles. Place the ruffles on the pillow top with right sides together, raw edges aligned, and the ends of ruffles ¼″ from the pillow corners. Baste in place.

6. Place the pillow back and top, right sides together, with ruffles tucked between them. Stitch, leaving a 5″ opening for turning. Clip the corners and turn right side out. Insert pillow form. Slipstitch the opening closed.

**Stitch Count: 112 x 112**

76

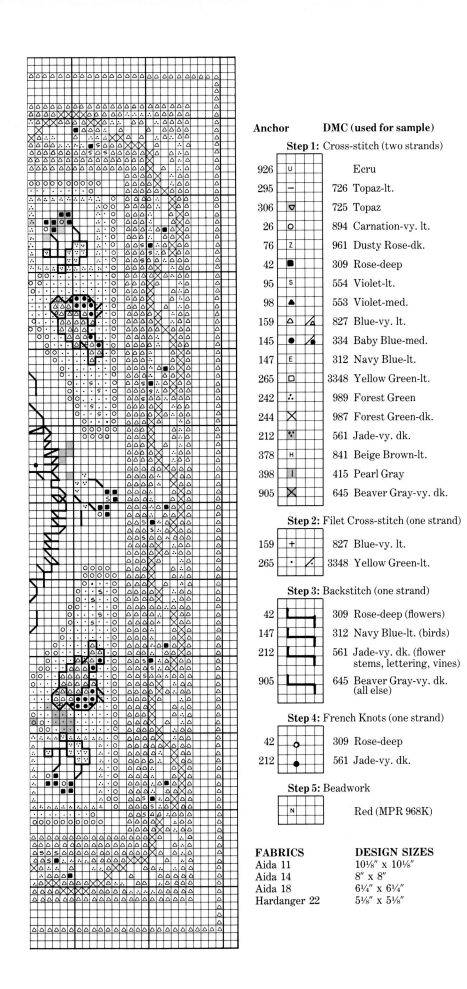

| Anchor | | | DMC (used for sample) |
|---|---|---|---|

**Step 1:** Cross-stitch (two strands)

| 926 | U | | Ecru |
|---|---|---|---|
| 295 | – | | 726 Topaz-lt. |
| 306 | ▽ | | 725 Topaz |
| 26 | O | | 894 Carnation-vy. lt. |
| 76 | Z | | 961 Dusty Rose-dk. |
| 42 | ■ | | 309 Rose-deep |
| 95 | S | | 554 Violet-lt. |
| 98 | ▲ | | 553 Violet-med. |
| 159 | △ | ╱ | 827 Blue-vy. lt. |
| 145 | ● | ╱ | 334 Baby Blue-med. |
| 147 | E | | 312 Navy Blue-lt. |
| 265 | ▢ | | 3348 Yellow Green-lt. |
| 242 | ∴ | | 989 Forest Green |
| 244 | ✕ | | 987 Forest Green-dk. |
| 212 | ⦂ | | 561 Jade-vy. dk. |
| 378 | H | | 841 Beige Brown-lt. |
| 398 | I | | 415 Pearl Gray |
| 905 | ✕ | | 645 Beaver Gray-vy. dk. |

**Step 2:** Filet Cross-stitch (one strand)

| 159 | + | | 827 Blue-vy. lt. |
|---|---|---|---|
| 265 | · | ╱ | 3348 Yellow Green-lt. |

**Step 3:** Backstitch (one strand)

| 42 | | 309 Rose-deep (flowers) |
|---|---|---|
| 147 | | 312 Navy Blue-lt. (birds) |
| 212 | | 561 Jade-vy. dk. (flower stems, lettering, vines) |
| 905 | | 645 Beaver Gray-vy. dk. (all else) |

**Step 4:** French Knots (one strand)

| 42 | ○ | 309 Rose-deep |
|---|---|---|
| 212 | ● | 561 Jade-vy. dk. |

**Step 5:** Beadwork

| | N | | Red (MPR 968K) |
|---|---|---|---|

**FABRICS**
**DESIGN SIZES**

| FABRICS | DESIGN SIZES |
|---|---|
| Aida 11 | 10⅛" x 10⅛" |
| Aida 14 | 8" x 8" |
| Aida 18 | 6¼" x 6¼" |
| Hardanger 22 | 5⅛" x 5⅛" |

## JULY 18–27
# *Frontier Days*

The world's oldest and best-known rodeo celebration takes place each year in Cheyenne, Wyoming, as the city revels in its reputation as a leading community of the Old West. The lone cowboy framed by the glowing sunset preserves our image of the adventurous life of the frontiersman. He's part of our heritage and hero to millions of today's children.

# *The Frontier*

## SAMPLE
Stitched on terra-cotta Lugana 25 over two threads, the finished design size is 13⅝″ x 8¾″. The fabric was cut 20″ x 15″.

| Anchor | | | DMC (used for sample) | |
|---|---|---|---|---|
| **Step 1: Cross-stitch (two strands)** | | | | |
| 386 | · | ⁄ | 746 | Off White |
| 301 | – | ⁄ | 744 | Yellow-pale |
| 303 | □ | | 742 | Tangerine-lt. |
| 316 | ✕ | | 740 | Tangerine |
| 332 | ▲ | | 946 | Burnt Orange-med. |
| 19 | B | | 817 | Coral Red-vy. dk. |
| 970 | ∴ | | 315 | Antique Mauve-dk. |
| 128 | + | | 800 | Delft-pale |
| 921 | N | ⁄ | 931 | Antique Blue-med. |
| 922 | O | | 930 | Antique Blue-dk. |
| 851 | ● | | 924 | Slate Green-vy. dk. |
| 324 | S | | 922 | Copper-lt. |
| 339 | H | | 920 | Copper-med. |
| 5968 | △ | ⁄ | 355 | Terra Cotta-dk. |
| 936 | ■ | ⁄ | 632 | Negro Flesh |
| 376 | Z | ⁄ | 842 | Beige Brown-vy. lt. |
| 379 | · | ⁄ | 840 | Beige Brown-med. |
| 380 | ▽ | ⁄ | 839 | Beige Brown-dk. |
| 381 | ∴ | ⁄ | 838 | Beige Brown-vy. dk. |
| 382 | ✕ | ⁄ | 3371 | Black Brown |
| 397 | ▨ | ⁄ | 762 | Pearl Gray-vy. lt. |
| 398 | I | | 415 | Pearl Gray |
| 399 | □ | | 318 | Steel Gray-lt. |

**Step 2: Backstitch (one strand)**

| 922 | 930 | Antique Blue-dk. (shirt, pants) |
|---|---|---|
| 382 | 3371 | Black Brown (all else) |

| FABRICS | DESIGN SIZES |
|---|---|
| Aida 11 | 15½″ x 10″ |
| Aida 14 | 12⅛″ x 7⅛″ |
| Aida 18 | 9½″ x 6⅛″ |
| Hardanger 22 | 7¾″ x 5″ |

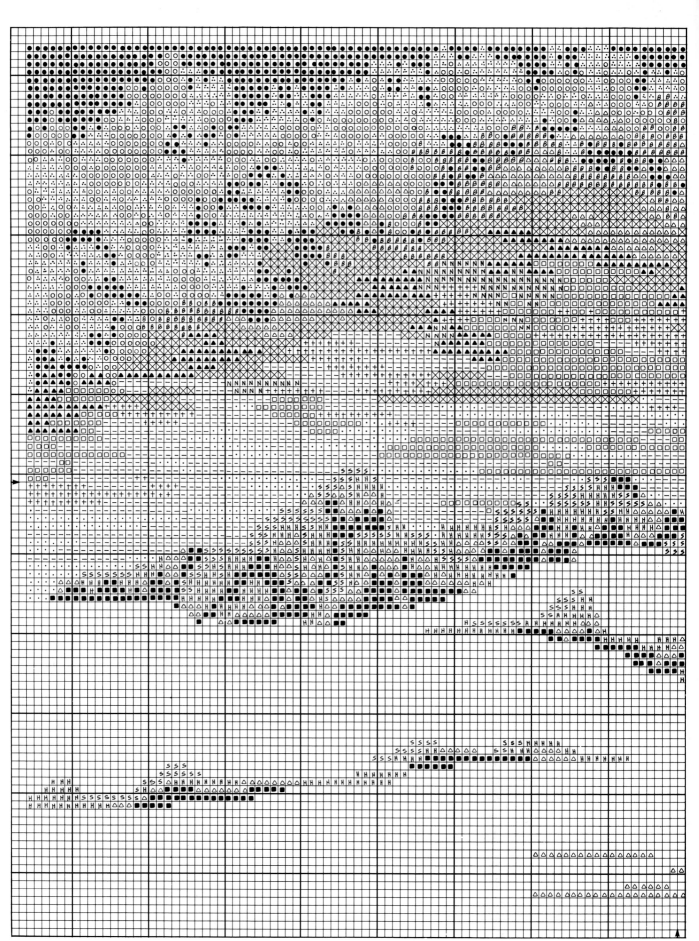

**Stitch Count: 170 x 110**

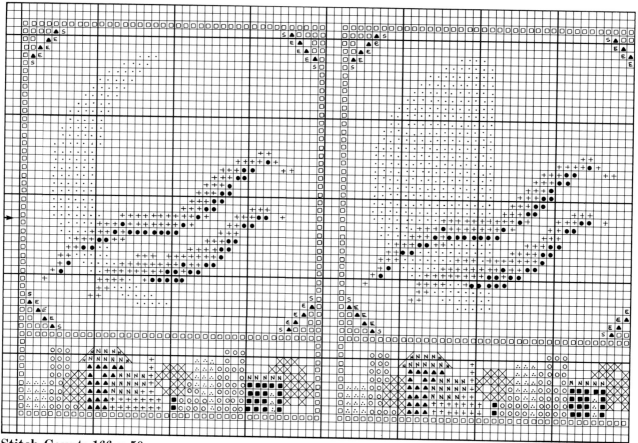

**Stitch Count: 166 x 50**

## JULY 20
*Moon Day*

Twenty years ago today, eyes across America were glued to television sets, as United States astronauts Neil Armstrong and Edwin "Buzz" Aldrin, Jr., landed and walked on the moon, taking "one small step for a man, one giant leap for mankind." Astronaut Michael Collins piloted the command module while Armstrong and Aldrin walked on the moon's surface. No longer is a trip to the moon just a flight of fancy!

# The Moon

**SAMPLE**
Stitched on black Hardanger 22 over two threads, the finished design size is 15⅛" x 4½". The fabric was cut 22" x 11".

| Anchor | | | DMC (used for sample) | |
|---|---|---|---|---|
| **Step 1:** Cross-stitch (three strands) | | | | |
| 1 | ∴ | | | White |
| 301 | · | ╱ | 744 | Yellow-pale |
| 297 | − | ╱ | 743 | Yellow-med. |
| 42 | ▲ | ◣ | 309 | Rose-deep |
| 119 | E | | 333 | Blue Violet-dk. |
| 159 | + | | 3325 | Baby Blue |
| 145 | S | | 334 | Baby Blue-med. |
| 921 | ● | | 931 | Antique Blue-med. |

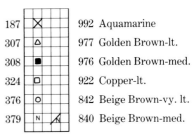

| Anchor | | | DMC | |
|---|---|---|---|---|
| 187 | ✕ | | 992 | Aquamarine |
| 307 | △ | | 977 | Golden Brown-lt. |
| 308 | ◼ | | 976 | Golden Brown-med. |
| 324 | ▢ | | 922 | Copper-lt. |
| 376 | ○ | | 842 | Beige Brown-vy. lt. |
| 379 | N | ╱ | 840 | Beige Brown-med. |

**Step 2:** Backstitch (one strand)

| 403 | ⌐ | | 310 | Black |
|---|---|---|---|---|

| FABRICS | DESIGN SIZES |
|---|---|
| Aida 11 | 15⅛" x 4½" |
| Aida 14 | 11⅞" x 3⅜" |
| Aida 18 | 9¼" x 2¾" |
| Hardanger 22 | 7½" x 2¼" |

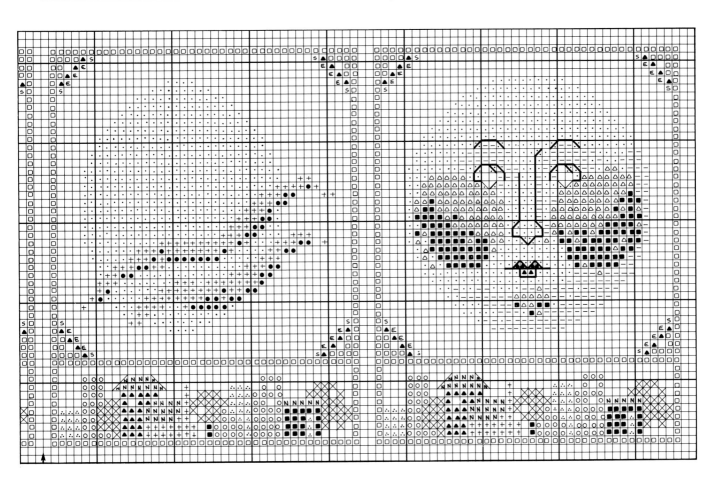

## AUGUST 1–7
# National Clown Week

Send in the clowns! No matter what their size or shape, the funny faces, clothes, and feet of these comical characters spread joy and laughter and rekindle the childlike wonder in us all. For that someone special, young or old, this cross-stitch pillow and quilt will be a delightful surprise.

# Pierrot Pillow

## SAMPLE
Stitched on white Hardanger 22 over two threads, the finished design size for one motif is 2¼" x 5". The fabric was cut 7" x 10". The finished pillow size is 15" x 18".

## MATERIALS
Completed cross-stitch on white
  Hardanger 22; matching thread
⅝ yard of 45"-wide black/white
  windowpane print fabric
½ yard of 45"-wide polyester
  fleece
½ yard of 45"-wide muslin
⅛ yard of 45"-wide white fabric
½ yard of 45"-wide burgundy
  pindot fabric
½ yard of 45"-wide black/white
  check fabric
Dressmakers' pen
Stuffing

## DIRECTIONS
All seam allowances are ¼". Press them away from the white fabric.

1. Cut the Hardanger 5" x 8" with the design centered. Zigzag the edges.

2. From windowpane fabric, cut one 15" x 18¼" piece for the back of the pillow. Also cut two 3½" x 6¾" pieces and two 3½" squares for the pillow top.

3. Cut the fleece 15" x 18¼". Cut a piece of muslin 15" x 18¼".

4. From white fabric, cut four 3½" squares and one 1⅛" x 9" strip.

5. From the pindot fabric, cut two 1⅛" x 19" and two 1⅛" x 15" strips for the sashing. Also cut one 2⅞" x 9" strip.

6. From the check fabric, cut two 2" x 19" and two 2" x 15" strips.

7. With right sides together, stitch the 1⅛″ x 9″ white strip to the 2⅞″ x 9″ pindot strip, along a 9″ edge. Cut across the white/pindot band every 1⅛″ to make eight strips.

8. With right sides together, stitch a white/pindot strip to two opposite sides of a windowpane square. Make sure that the white/pindot sections are positioned the same on both sides of the square. Repeat, using the second windowpane square and two additional white/pindot strips. Stitch the remaining white/pindot strips to the 3½″ ends of the rectangular windowpane pieces.

9. To complete Row 1 and Row 3 of the pillow, pin white squares to the strips on the sides of the windowpane squares, right sides together. Stitch (Diagram A).

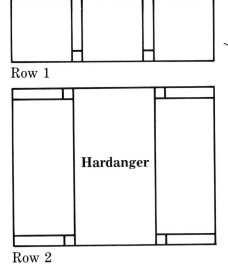

Row 1

Row 2

**Hardanger**

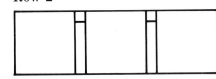

Row 3

**Diagram A**

10. To complete Row 2, pin a long side of the rectangular windowpane blocks (white squares toward

Hardanger) to each side of the stitched design, right sides together. Stitch (Diagram A).

11. With right sides together, stitch the three rows to one another (stitched design in the center and small white squares toward Hardanger).

12. Stitch the long edges of the pindot sashing and check border strips together. Mark the centers of the bands on the pindot fabric and the centers of the outside edges of the pillow top.

13. With right sides together, pin the four bands to the pillow top, matching the centers. Stitch around the entire edge, stitching to within ¼″ of the corners.

14. To miter the corners, fold two adjacent strips with right sides together and stitch at a 45° angle (Diagram B). Trim the seam allowance to ¼″.

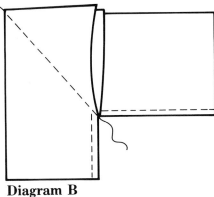

**Diagram B**

15. Stack the muslin, fleece, and pillow top (right side up). Baste the three layers together securely. Machine-quilt on all seam lines.

16. With right sides together, pin the pieced pillow top to the back. Stitch, leaving an opening in the bottom edge for turning. Clip the corners and turn. Stuff firmly. Slipstitch the opening closed.

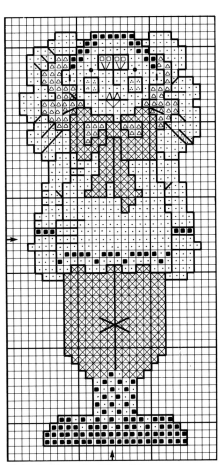

**Stitch Count: 25 x 55**

| Anchor | | DMC (used for sample) |
|---|---|---|
| | | **Step 1:** Cross-stitch (three strands) |
| 1 | · | White |
| 4146 | △ | 754 Peach Flesh-lt. |
| 8 | ∴ | 761 Salmon-lt. |
| 897 | X | 221 Shell Pink-dk. |
| 128 | ▢ | 800 Delft-pale |
| 403 | ■ | 310 Black |

| | | **Step 2:** Backstitch |
|---|---|---|
| 74 | ∨∨ | 3354 Dusty Rose-lt., two strands (mouth) |
| 400 | ∨ | 414 Steel Gray-dk., two strands (eyes) |
| 403 | ⌐ | 310 Black, one strand (all else except wrinkles in pants and collar) |

| | | **Step 3:** Long Stitch (one strand) |
|---|---|---|
| 403 | ╱ | 310 Black (wrinkles in pants and collar) |

| | | **Step 4:** French Knots (one strand) |
|---|---|---|
| 403 | ● | 310 Black |

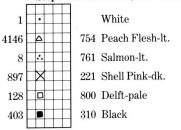

| FABRICS | DESIGN SIZES |
|---|---|
| Aida 11 | 2¼″ x 5″ |
| Aida 14 | 1¾″ x 3⅞″ |
| Aida 18 | 1⅜″ x 3″ |
| Hardanger 22 | 1⅛″ x 2½″ |

# *Pierrot Quilt*

**SAMPLE**

Stitched on white Hardanger 22 over two threads, the design was repeated five times with 2⅛″ between designs. Center the first design on the fabric; then repeat the design on either side of the first design. The fabric was cut 24″ x 10″. The finished quilt size is 38″ x 57½″.

**MATERIALS**

Completed cross-stitch on white Hardanger 22; matching thread
⅜ yard of 45″-wide black/white check fabric
¼ yard of 45″-wide burgundy pindot fabric
3½ yards of 45″-wide white fabric
½ yard of 45″-wide black/white windowpane fabric
¼ yard of 45″-wide black fabric; matching thread
½ yard of ⅛″-wide black/white polka-dot grosgrain ribbon
Dressmakers' pen
Fusible web

**DIRECTIONS**

All seam allowances are ¼″. Press them away from white fabric.

**1.** Cut the Hardanger 21¾″ x 8″ with the design centered. Zigzag the edges.

**2.** From black/white check fabric, cut two 1½″ x 33″ and two 1½″ x 19″ strips for the sashing for the upper section of the quilt.

**3.** From burgundy pindot fabric, cut two 1⅛″ x 33″ and two 1⅛″ x 19″ strips, also for the upper section of the quilt. Cut additional 1⅛″-wide strips to equal at least 68″.

**4.** From white fabric, cut a 38″ x 58″ piece for the backing; set aside. Cut a 28½″ square for the lower section of the quilt. Cut 1⅛″-wide white strips to equal at least 42″. Cut additional strips: one 3″ x 30½″, two 3½″ x 16¾″, four 3½″ x 30½″. Cut 3″-wide white bias strips for binding, piecing as needed, to equal 5½ yards. Also cut four 3″ squares.

**5.** From windowpane fabric, cut four 1½″ x 33″ strips for the sashing in the lower section of the quilt. Also cut ten 3″ squares and two 3″ x 6¼″ rectangles.

**6.** From the black fabric, cut four 3½″ squares and two 3″ x 3½″ pieces. Save the remaining black fabric for the star.

**7.** For Section 1, stitch a 3½″ black square to each end of a 3½″ x 30½″ white strip (Diagram C). Set aside.

**8.** For Section 2, sew the long edges of the pindot and the long edges of the white 1⅛″-wide strips together, piecing as needed, to equal 35″. Cut across the band every 1⅛″ to make eight strips. Then cut eight 2⅞″ strips. Turn the long strips so that you have white fabric on the right-hand side of four units and white on the left side of the other four. Stitch the 1⅛″ strips to one end of the 2⅞″ strips, matching seams and reversing fabrics so that the white square abuts the pindot strip and the pindot square abuts the white strip.

**9.** From the remaining pindot strips, cut eight 2⅞″ segments. From the remaining white strips, cut eight 1⅛″ segments. Stitch the pindot and white pieces together.

**10.** To form Row 1 of Section 2, sew four of the double white/pindot units between the five windowpane squares. Stitch the single white/pindot units to the outside edges of the end squares. Then sew a white square to each end of the row. Repeat for Row 3 of Section 2 (Diagram C).

**11.** For the center row of Section 2, stitch a single white/pindot strip to each end of each windowpane rectangle. Stitch one windowpane unit to each end of the stitched design.

**12.** Positioning the small white squares so that they are next to the Hardanger, pin the three rows, right sides together and seams matching. Stitch.

**13.** Matching centers, stitch the long edges of the pindot and check sashing strips together. Mark the centers of the four edges of Section 2 and the centers of the sashing strips. Matching centers, attach the strips, stitching to within ¼″ of the corners.

**14.** To miter the corners, fold two adjacent strips with right sides together and stitch at a 45° angle (Diagram B). Trim seam allowance. Repeat with remaining corners.

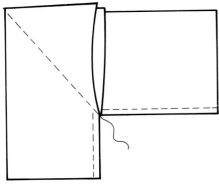

**Diagram B**

**15.** Complete Section 2 by sewing a 3½″ x 16¾″ white strip to each side (Diagram C).

**16.** For Section 3, sew a 3″ x 3½″ black piece to each end of the 3″ x 30½″ white strip (Diagram C).

**17.** For Section 4, mark the centers of the edges of the four windowpane sashing strips. Also mark the center of each side of the 28½″ white square. Attach the sashing as you did in Steps 13 and 14.

**18.** Stitch a 3½″ x 30½″ white strip to each side of the large section (Diagram C).

**19.** For Section 5, stitch a 3½″ black square to each end of a 3½″ x 30½″ white strip (Diagram C).

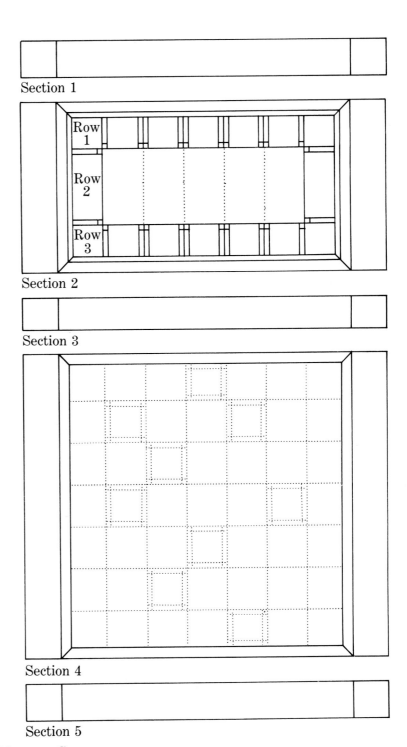

Section 1

Section 2

Section 3

Section 4

Section 5

**Diagram C**

**20.** With right sides together, sew the five sections to one another, matching seams.

**21.** Mark quilting lines at 4¼″ intervals on Hardanger between the clown motifs. Quilting lines should align with the seams between the white/pindot strips. Also mark quilting lines in a grid pattern on the lower section (Diagram C).

The quilting lines inside the quilted squares are ½″ from and parallel to the grid lines.

**22.** Stitch the ribbon over the second grid line from the right.

**23.** Trace the pattern for the star onto fusible web. Fuse to the black fabric, following the manufacturer's instructions. Cut out the star and fuse it to the quilt top, covering the ribbon end. Satin-stitch the edge of the star.

**24.** Stack the quilt backing, right side down; fleece; and quilt top, right side up. Baste the three layers together securely. Quilt by machine on the seam lines between the windowpane blocks in the upper section, around the edge of the Hardanger, on the quilting lines between clowns, and on the seam lines of both sashings. Continue to quilt on the seam lines and the marked grid. Also quilt beside the ribbon and around the star.

**25.** Trim the entire border, through all layers, 3½″ from and parallel to the sashing.

**26.** Fold the white bias strip in half so it is 1½″ wide. Stitch the bias strip to the right side of the quilt with a ½″ seam, matching the raw edges. To miter a corner, stop ½″ from the edge of the corner and backstitch (Diagram D). Fold the bias strip at the edge and turn the corner. Resume stitching with a backstitch ½″ from the adjacent edge (Diagram E). Repeat for remaining corners. Fold the bias to the back of the quilt and slipstitch.

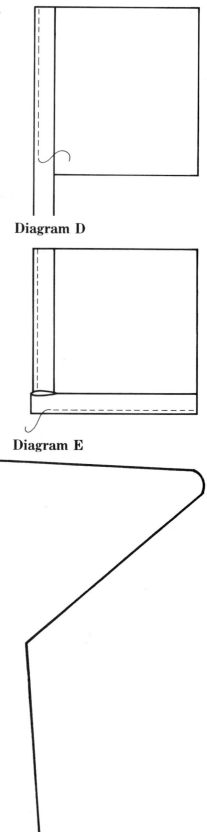

**Diagram D**

**Diagram E**

**Star Pattern**

88

## AUGUST 12
# *Railroaders' Festival*

All aboard! The glorious "good old days" of railroading are celebrated annually in Promontory, Utah, with professional spike-driving contests, pole sliding, and handcar races. This handbill recalls our nation's romance with the railroad.

# Go by Train

**SAMPLE**
Stitched on Rustico 14, the finished design size is 7" x 15⅜". The fabric was cut 13" x 22".

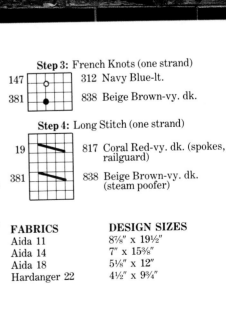

**Anchor**　　**DMC (used for sample)**

**Step 1:** Cross-stitch (two strands)

| Anchor | | DMC | |
|---|---|---|---|
| 387 | + | 712 | Cream |
| 306 | | 725 | Topaz |
| 891 | | 676 | Old Gold-lt. |
| 347 | X | 402 | Mahogany-vy. lt. |
| 323 | H | 722 | Orange Spice-lt. |
| 11 | △ | 350 | Coral-med. |
| 19 | ● | 817 | Coral Red-vy. dk. |
| 167 | - | 598 | Turquoise-lt. |
| 168 | ○ | 807 | Peacock Blue |
| 161 | □ | 826 | Blue-med. |
| 147 | ■ | 312 | Navy Blue-lt. |
| 265 | | 3348 | Yellow Green-lt. |
| 215 | ▢ | 320 | Pistachio Green-med. |
| 216 | ▲ | 367 | Pistachio Green-dk. |
| 309 | ○ | 435 | Brown-vy. lt. |

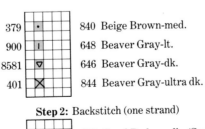

| | | | |
|---|---|---|---|
| 379 | • | 840 | Beige Brown-med. |
| 900 | I | 648 | Beaver Gray-lt. |
| 8581 | ▽ | 646 | Beaver Gray-dk. |
| 401 | X | 844 | Beaver Gray-ultra dk. |

**Step 2:** Backstitch (one strand)

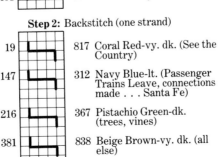

| | | | |
|---|---|---|---|
| 19 | | 817 | Coral Red-vy. dk. (See the Country) |
| 147 | | 312 | Navy Blue-lt. (Passenger Trains Leave, connections made . . . Santa Fe) |
| 216 | | 367 | Pistachio Green-dk. (trees, vines) |
| 381 | | 838 | Beige Brown-vy. dk. (all else) |

**Step 3:** French Knots (one strand)

| | | | |
|---|---|---|---|
| 147 | ○ | 312 | Navy Blue-lt. |
| 381 | ● | 838 | Beige Brown-vy. dk. |

**Step 4:** Long Stitch (one strand)

| | | | |
|---|---|---|---|
| 19 | | 817 | Coral Red-vy. dk. (spokes, railguard) |
| 381 | | 838 | Beige Brown-vy. dk. (steam poofer) |

**FABRICS**　　　**DESIGN SIZES**

| FABRICS | DESIGN SIZES |
|---|---|
| Aida 11 | 8⅞" x 19½" |
| Aida 14 | 7" x 15⅜" |
| Aida 18 | 5⅛" x 12" |
| Hardanger 22 | 4½" x 9¾" |

90

**Stitch Count: 98 x 215**

## SEPTEMBER 22
### *First Day of Autumn*

Autumn hues fascinate our eyes as we watch green turn magically into vibrant shades of yellow, orange, and red. Gathered together in our fall pillow for Celebration of the Seasons, these colors reflect the season of harvest and home.

# *Autumn Pillow*

### SAMPLE
Stitched on driftwood Belfast Linen 32 over two threads, the finished design size is 7″ x 7″. The fabric was cut 17″ x 17″.

### MATERIALS
Completed cross-stitch on driftwood Belfast Linen 32; matching thread
¾ yard of 45″-wide yellow fabric
2 yards of purchased tan bias tape; matching thread
Dressmakers' pen
14″ knife-edge pillow form

### DIRECTIONS
All seam allowances are ¼″.

1. With the design centered, cut a 13½″ square from the linen.

2. Cut one 13½″ square from yellow fabric for the pillow backing. Also cut four 5″ x 17″ bias strips for ruffles.

3. Draw a line down the lengthwise center of each strip. Place the raw edge of the bias tape next to the line, right sides together, and stitch ¼″ from the edge. Fold the tape back over the line and, keeping the tape smooth, topstitch it to the strip. Repeat with the remaining strips.

4. Fold one strip with right sides together to measure 2½″ wide; stitch the ends. Turn right side out. Press the strip with the fold in the center of the bias tape. Repeat with the three remaining strips.

5. Stitch a gathering thread close to the raw edges of one strip. Gather slightly to 13″; repeat for remaining strips to make four ruffles. Place the ruffles on the pillow top with right sides together, raw edges aligned, and the ends of the ruffles ¼″ from the pillow corners. Baste in place.

6. Place the pillow back and top, right sides together, with ruffles tucked between them. Stitch, leaving a 5″ opening for turning. Clip the corners and turn right side out. Insert pillow form. Slipstitch the opening closed.

**Stitch Count: 112 x 112**

94

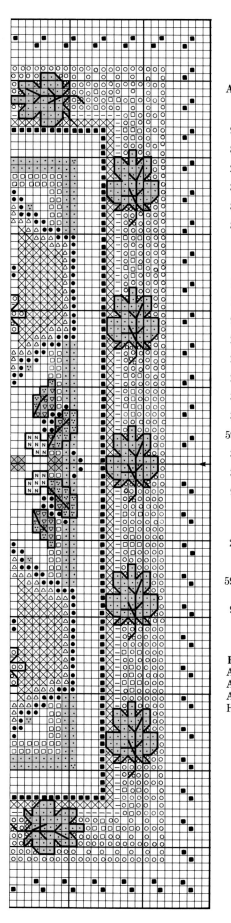

| Anchor | | | DMC (used for sample) | |
|---|---|---|---|---|
| | | | **Step 1:** Cross-stitch (two strands) | |
| 926 | U | | | Ecru |
| 886 | · | ⁄ | 677 | Old Gold-vy. lt. |
| 295 | + | | 726 | Topaz-lt. |
| 306 | ∴ | | 725 | Topaz |
| 881 | X | ⁄ | 945 | Sportsman Flesh |
| 868 | − | ⁄ | 758 | Terra Cotta-lt. |
| 9 | ▽ | | 760 | Salmon |
| 13 | ⁖ | | 347 | Salmon-dk. |
| 158 | · | | 747 | Sky Blue-vy. lt. |
| 168 | ▲ | | 597 | Turquoise |
| 920 | X | | 932 | Antique Blue-lt. |
| 264 | ▢ | ⁄ | 472 | Avocado Green-ultra lt. |
| 214 | △ | | 368 | Pistachio Green-lt. |
| 246 | ● | ⁄ | 319 | Pistachio Green-vy. dk. |
| 347 | ■ | | 402 | Mahogany-vy. lt. |
| 349 | N | | 921 | Copper |
| 5968 | ○ | ⁄ | 355 | Terra Cotta-dk. |
| 379 | I | | 840 | Beige Brown-med. |
| 398 | Z | | 415 | Pearl Gray |
| 905 | E | | 645 | Beaver Gray-vy. dk. |

**Step 2:** Backstitch (one strand)

| 246 | 319 Pistachio Green-vy. dk. (outer leaves, red leaves, Autumn) |
|---|---|
| 5968 | 355 Terra Cotta-dk. (terra cotta leaves) |
| 905 | 645 Beaver Gray-vy. dk. (all else) |

| FABRICS | DESIGN SIZES |
|---|---|
| Aida 11 | 10⅛" x 10⅛" |
| Aida 14 | 8" x 8" |
| Aida 18 | 6¼" x 6¼" |
| Hardanger 22 | 5⅛" x 5⅛" |

# SEPTEMBER 30
# Rosh Hashanah

Rosh Hashanah, the Jewish New Year, marks the beginning of the Jewish High Holy Days—a time for meditation and penitence. It is traditional at this time to dip slices of apple and challah bread in honey while wishing for a sweet and happy new year. This design says, "shalom," the Hebrew word for "peace," which is both a greeting and a farewell.

## *Jewish New Year*

**SAMPLE**
Stitched on blue Glenshee Linen 29 over two threads, the finished design size is 10¼" x 7¼". The fabric was cut 17" x 14".

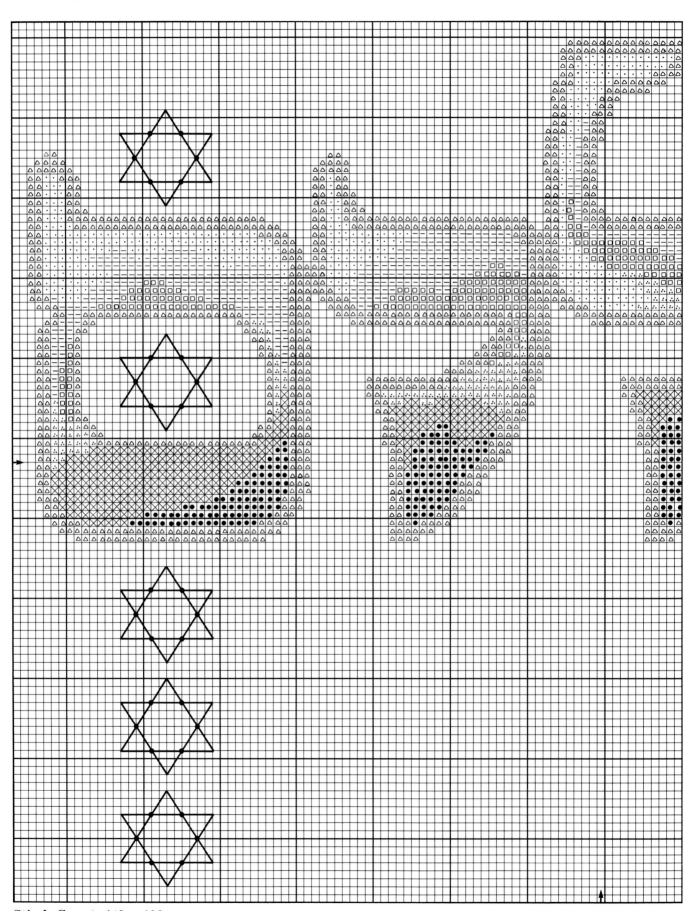

**Stitch Count: 149 x 106**

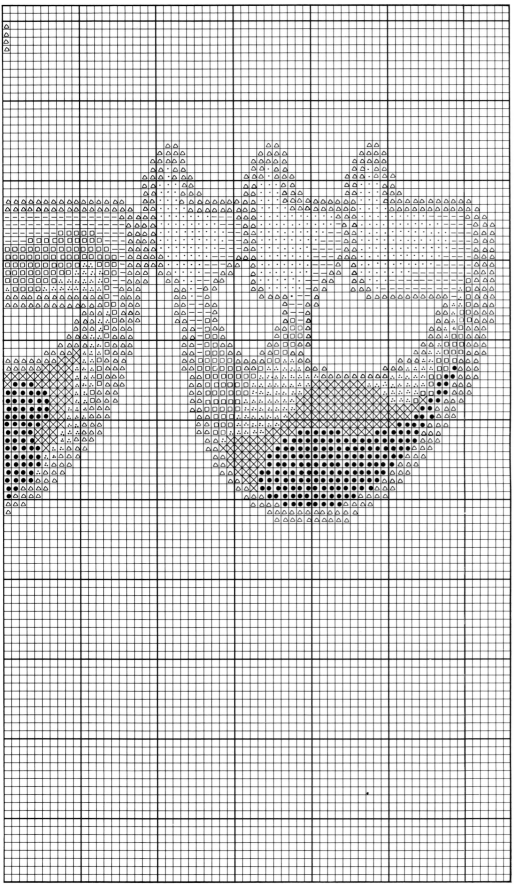

## OCTOBER 1
# *World Vegetarian Day*

Mother really does know best when she tells you to "eat your vegetables!" Remind your family of the health benefits of vegetables by planting our cross-stitch designs in your kitchen.

# *Vegetables*

**SAMPLES**

**Peas:** Stitched on white Aida 14, the finished design size is 4¾" x 6¾". The fabric was cut 11" x 13".

| Anchor | | DMC (used for sample) |
|---|---|---|
| **Step 1:** Cross-stitch (two strands) | | |
| 386 | · | 746 Off White |
| 886 | + | 677 Old Gold-vy. lt. |
| 891 | △ | 676 Old Gold-lt. |
| 890 | ■ | 729 Old Gold-med. |
| 264 | ∴ | 772 Pine Green-lt. |
| 256 | − | 704 Chartreuse-bright |
| 239 | □ | 702 Kelly Green |
| 229 | × | 700 Christmas Green-bright |

| | | |
|---|---|---|
| **Step 2:** Backstitch (one strand) | | |
| 403 | | 310 Black |

| | | |
|---|---|---|
| **Step 3:** French Knots (one strand) | | |
| 403 | ● | 310 Black |

| FABRICS | DESIGN SIZES |
|---|---|
| Aida 11 | 6" x 8⅝" |
| Aida 18 | 3⅝" x 5¼" |
| Hardanger 22 | 3" x 4⅜" |

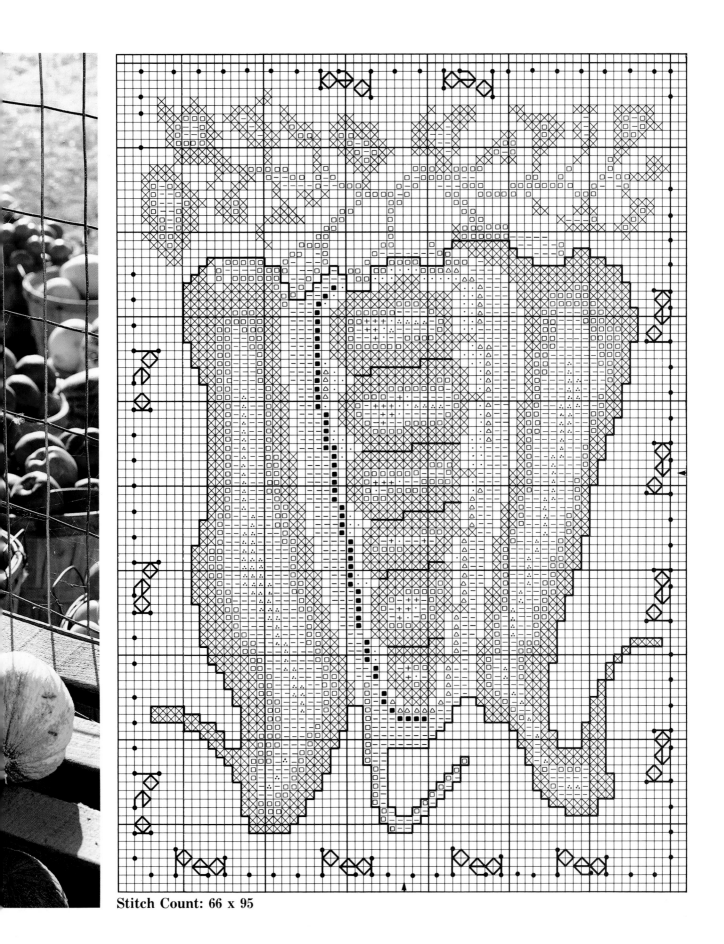

**Stitch Count: 66 x 95**

**Beet:** Stitched on white Aida 14, the finished design size is 4¾" x 6¾". The fabric was cut 11" x 13".

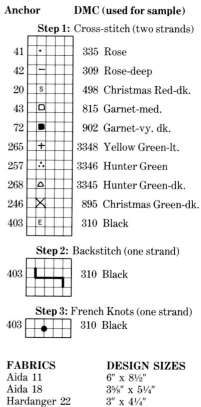

| Anchor | | DMC (used for sample) |
|---|---|---|

**Step 1:** Cross-stitch (two strands)

| Anchor | | DMC | |
|---|---|---|---|
| 41 | · | 335 | Rose |
| 42 | – | 309 | Rose-deep |
| 20 | s | 498 | Christmas Red-dk. |
| 43 | □ | 815 | Garnet-med. |
| 72 | ■ | 902 | Garnet-vy. dk. |
| 265 | + | 3348 | Yellow Green-lt. |
| 257 | ∴ | 3346 | Hunter Green |
| 268 | △ | 3345 | Hunter Green-dk. |
| 246 | ✕ | 895 | Christmas Green-dk. |
| 403 | E | 310 | Black |

**Step 2:** Backstitch (one strand)

| 403 | ⌐ | 310 | Black |
|---|---|---|---|

**Step 3:** French Knots (one strand)

| 403 | ● | 310 | Black |
|---|---|---|---|

| FABRICS | DESIGN SIZES |
|---|---|
| Aida 11 | 6" x 8½" |
| Aida 18 | 3⅝" x 5¼" |
| Hardanger 22 | 3" x 4¼" |

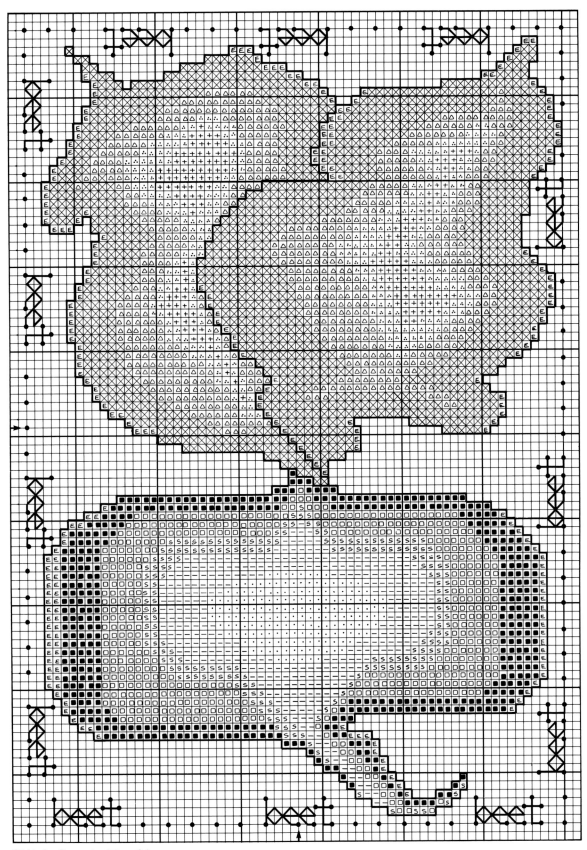

**Stitch Count: 66 x 94**

# OCTOBER 31
## *Halloween*

Pint-size ghosts and goblins will be spooking the neighborhood on this magical eve, to scare up bags full of candy treats. Keep your little spook warm this Halloween night with our sweatshirt, cross-stitched in ghostly fashion.

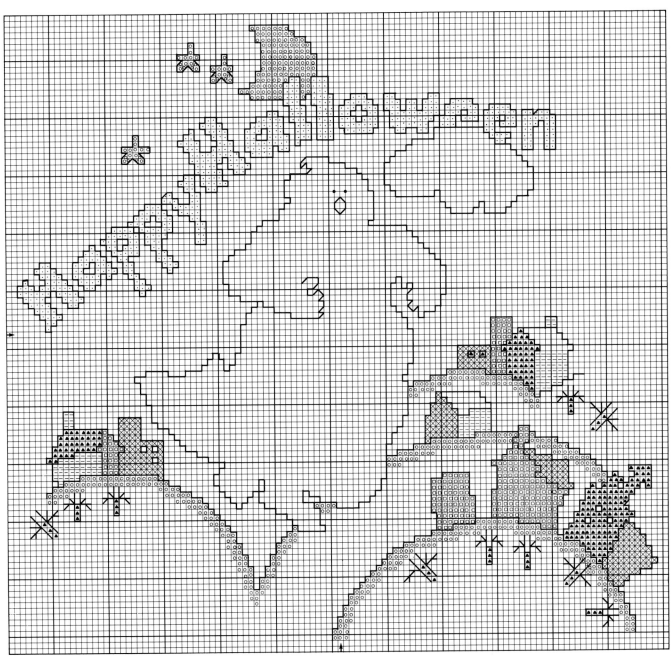

**Stitch Count: 115 x 107**

# *Sweatshirt*

**SAMPLE**

Stitched on a child's purchased medium white sweatshirt using Waste Canvas 14. The finished design size is 8¼" x 7⅝". The waste canvas was cut 13" x 12".

| Anchor | | | DMC (used for sample) |
|---|---|---|---|
| | | | **Step 1:** Cross-stitch (two strands) |
| 297 | O | ◿ | 743 Yellow-med. |
| 304 | • | ⟋ | 741 Tangerine-med. |
| 130 | □ | | 809 Delft |
| 131 | ✕ | | 798 Delft-dk. |
| 133 | ▲ | ◣ | 796 Royal Blue-dk. |
| 920 | − | | 932 Antique Blue-lt. |

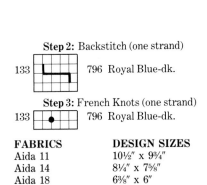

**Step 2:** Backstitch (one strand)

133     796 Royal Blue-dk.

**Step 3:** French Knots (one strand)

133     796 Royal Blue-dk.

| FABRICS | DESIGN SIZES |
|---|---|
| Aida 11 | 10½" x 9¾" |
| Aida 14 | 8¼" x 7⅝" |
| Aida 18 | 6⅜" x 6" |
| Hardanger 22 | 5¼" x 4⅞" |

# NOVEMBER 23
# *Thanksgiving*

The traditional get-together of family and friends on Thanksgiving Day is a time to rejoice in our bounty and blessings. It is a time to reflect on our history—a history filled with people reaching out to help others. It is a time to give thanks and a time to give of ourselves.

## *Holiday Table Runner*

### SAMPLE
Stitched on white Aida 14, the finished design size is 5⅞" x 2⅜". The fabric was cut 13" x 32". Center the stitched design 2" from one 11" edge of the fabric.

### MATERIALS
Completed cross-stitch on white
  Aida 14; matching thread
½ yard of 45"-wide white fabric
  for backing
½ yard of 45"-wide dark green
  pindot fabric for binding;
  matching thread
¼ yard of 45"-wide light green
  print fabric for border
⅛ yard of 45"-wide cinnamon
  chintz fabric for sashing
Small pieces of black print fabric
  for corners

2½ yards of ⅛″-wide apricot satin ribbon; matching embroidery floss
Dressmakers' pen
Material for template

**DIRECTIONS**
All seam allowances are ¼″.

**1.** Cut the Aida 11″ x 30″, with the designs centered 1¼″ from one 11″ edge.

**2.** Cut a 13¾″ x 32¾″ piece of white fabric for the backing. Cut a 1″-wide bias strip from the dark green fabric, piecing as needed, to equal 2½″ yards.

**3.** Cut two 1¼″ x 33½″ strips and two 1¼″ x 14½″ strips from light green fabric for the border.

**4.** Cut two 1⅛″ x 30″ strips and two 1⅛″ x 12″ strips from the cinnamon fabric for the sashing.

**5.** Trace and cut out the pattern for the corner triangle. Adding a ¼″ seam allowance, cut four corner triangles from black print fabric.

**6.** With right sides together, pin the 30″ cinnamon sashing strips to the 30″ sides of the design piece. Stitch. Pin the 12″ sashing strips across the ends, crossing the 30″ strips. Stitch. Trim the excess.

**Corner Triangle Pattern**

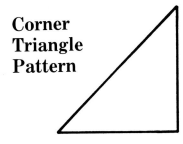

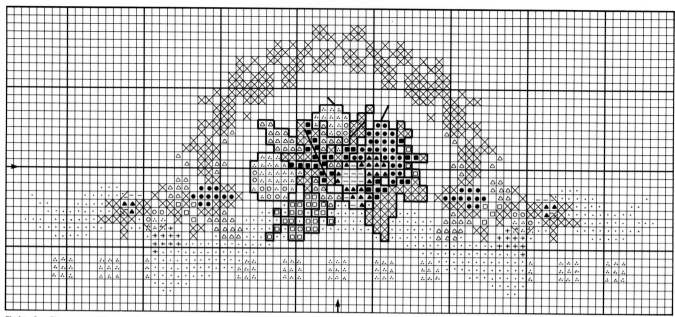

**Stitch Count: 83 x 34**

**7.** Turn the table runner right side up and place the triangle pattern in one corner. Draw a line next to the long edge of the triangle. With right sides together, pin a fabric triangle to the corner of the table runner, aligning the long edge of the triangle with the line drawn on the table runner. Stitch on the stitching line (Diagram A). Trim the seam and flip triangle back to match the corner and cover the sashing. Repeat with the remaining corners.

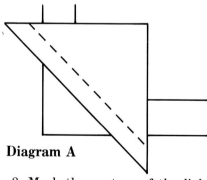

**Diagram A**

**8.** Mark the centers of the light green border strips and cinnamon sashing strips. With right sides together and centers matching, pin long border strips to the long edges of the sashing strips. Stitch to within ¼″ of each corner; backstitch. Repeat with short border strips.

**9.** To miter the corners, fold the right sides of two adjacent strips together and stitch at a 45° angle (Diagram B). Trim the seam allowance to ¼″. Repeat for the remaining corners.

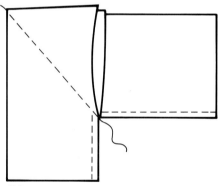

**Diagram B**

**10.** Cut two 12″ pieces of ribbon; cut the remaining ribbon in half. Place one long piece of ribbon ½″ inside the long edge of the Aida. Using one strand of floss, couch with cross-stitches. Stitch over two threads, leaving two threads between stitches, stopping 1″ from the corners. Repeat on the opposite long edge and then the short edges, overlapping the ends of the long ribbon pieces (see photo). Secure the overlapped ribbon corners with a single cross-stitch. Trim the ribbon ends.

**11.** With wrong sides together, pin the top of the table runner to the white backing fabric. Trim the backing to match the top; baste. With right sides together and raw edges aligned, pin the bias binding to the design piece. Stitch through all layers. Fold the binding double to the back and slipstitch.

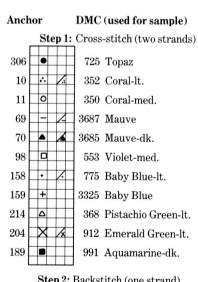

| Anchor | | | DMC (used for sample) | |
|---|---|---|---|---|
| **Step 1:** Cross-stitch (two strands) | | | | |
| 306 | ● | | 725 | Topaz |
| 10 | ∴ | ◸ | 352 | Coral-lt. |
| 11 | O | | 350 | Coral-med. |
| 69 | − | ◸ | 3687 | Mauve |
| 70 | ▲ | ◤ | 3685 | Mauve-dk. |
| 98 | ▫ | | 553 | Violet-med. |
| 158 | · | ◸ | 775 | Baby Blue-lt. |
| 159 | + | | 3325 | Baby Blue |
| 214 | △ | | 368 | Pistachio Green-lt. |
| 204 | ✕ | ◹ | 912 | Emerald Green-lt. |
| 189 | ■ | | 991 | Aquamarine-dk. |
| **Step 2:** Backstitch (one strand) | | | | |
| 149 | | | 336 | Navy Blue |

**FABRICS**
Aida 11
Aida 18
Hardanger 22

**DESIGN SIZES**
7½″ x 3⅛″
4⅝″ x 1⅞″
3¾″ x 1½″

# Napkin Rings & Napkins

## SAMPLES

Stitched on white Aida 14, using outer wreath of one wall hanging graph. Finished design size for each wreath is 3¾″ x 3¾″. For each ring, fabric was cut in an 8″ square.

## MATERIALS (for two rings and two napkins)

Completed cross-stitch for two napkin rings on white Aida 14; matching thread

Two 5″ squares of white fabric for backing

Two 5″ squares of polyester fleece

Small amount of dark green pin-dot fabric; matching thread

½ yard of 45″-wide light green print fabric for napkins

Dressmakers' pen

## DIRECTIONS

All seam allowances are ¼″.

1. Trace and cut out the pattern for the napkin ring. Cut one ring from each Aida piece with designs centered. Cut two rings from white fabric and two from fleece.

2. Cut a ¾″-wide bias strip from dark green fabric, piecing as needed, to equal 1¼ yards.

3. Pin one fleece ring to wrong side of one Aida ring. Fold bias strip in half, wrong sides together. With raw edges aligned, stitch folded strip to front of one Aida ring along outside and inside edges, overlapping ends. Trim fleece. Repeat for second ring.

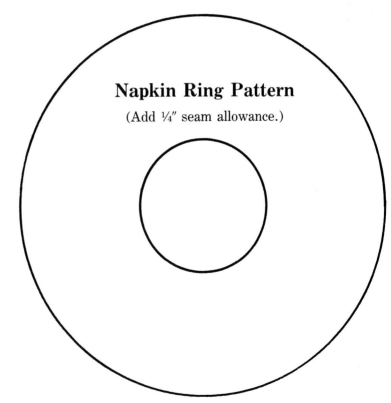

**Napkin Ring Pattern**

(Add ¼″ seam allowance.)

4. With right sides together, stitch the top of the napkin ring to the back, along the outside edge only. Turn right side out. Clip the inside seam allowance. Slipstitch the inside edge. Repeat to make the second napkin ring.

5. For napkins, cut two 16″ squares from light green fabric. Machine-satin-stitch around all edges, using dark green thread. Trim the excess fabric from the stitching. Stitch the edges again.

| Anchor | DMC (used for sample) | | |
|--------|--|--|--|

**Step 1: Cross-stitch (two strands)**

| 300 | – | | 745 | Yellow-lt. pale |
|-----|---|---|-----|----------------|
| 306 | ● | | 725 | Topaz |
| 10 | ∴ | ◣ | 352 | Coral-lt. |
| 11 | ○ | ◪ | 350 | Coral-med. |
| 48 | + | ◪ | 818 | Baby Pink |
| 98 | H | | 553 | Violet-med. |
| 159 | ▢ | ◪ | 827 | Blue-vy. lt. |
| 161 | E | | 826 | Blue-med. |
| 203 | • | ◪ | 954 | Nile Green |
| 204 | ✕ | | 912 | Emerald Green-lt. |
| 228 | ▲ | | 910 | Emerald Green-dk. |
| 214 | △ | ◪ | 368 | Pistachio Green-lt. |
| 189 | ■ | ◣ | 991 | Aquamarine-dk. |
| 889 | B | | 610 | Drab Brown-vy. dk. |

**Stitch Count: 52 x 52**

**Step 2:** Backstitch (one strand)

| 161 | | 826 Blue-med. (lettering) |
| --- | --- | --- |
| 149 | | 336 Navy Blue (all else) |

**Step 3:** Beadwork

| S | | Pale Peach (MPR 148T) |
| --- | --- | --- |
| U | | Robin's Egg Blue (MPR 143T) |

**FABRICS**      **DESIGN SIZES**
Aida 11      4³⁄₄" x 4³⁄₄"
Aida 18      2⁷⁄₈" x 2⁷⁄₈"
Hardanger 22      2³⁄₈" x 2³⁄₈"

# Wall Hanging

## SAMPLE
Stitched on white Aida 14, the finished design size for each wreath is 3¾" x 3¾". The fabric was cut in an 8" square for each design block.

## MATERIALS
Four completed cross-stitch designs on Aida 14: matching thread
¾ yard of 45"-wide dark green pindot fabric; matching thread
¼ yard of 45"-wide cinnamon chintz fabric for sashing
¼ yard of 45"-wide light green print for sashing
Small pieces of black print for corners
⅝ yard of 45"-wide polyester fleece
Dressmakers' pen
Material for template

## DIRECTIONS
All seam allowances are ¼".

**1.** Cut the Aida in four 5¾" squares with the designs centered.

**2.** Cut one 19" square of dark green fabric for the backing and two 2½" x 36" strips for the ties. Also cut four 2¼" x 15¾" pieces for the border strips.

**3.** Cut five 1¼" x 16" strips and two 1¼" x 7" strips from light green fabric for sashing.

**4.** Cut four 2¼" squares from cinnamon chintz. Also cut eight 1⅛" x 5¾" strips and eight 1⅛" x 6½" strips for sashing.

**5.** Trace and cut out the pattern for the corner triangle. Cut sixteen corner triangles from black print fabric, adding ¼" seam allowance.

**6.** Stitch 5¾" strips of cinnamon fabric to two opposite sides of one design piece. Repeat with the remaining design pieces. Stitch a 6½" strip to the top and bottom of one design piece. Repeat with remaining design pieces.

**7.** Turn one design piece right side up and place the triangle pattern in one corner. Draw a line next to the long edge of the triangle. With right sides together, pin a fabric triangle to the corner of the design piece, aligning the long edge of the triangle with the line drawn on the design piece. Stitch on the stitching line (Diagram A). Trim the seam and flip the triangle back to match the corner and cover the sashing. Repeat with remaining corners for all the design pieces.

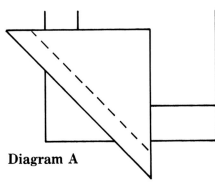

**Diagram A**

**8.** Position the design pieces as shown in photo. With right sides together, pin the long edges of one 1¼" x 7" light green strip between two design pieces and stitch (Diagram B); repeat with remaining two designs.

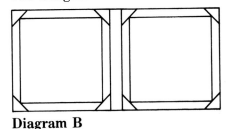

**Diagram B**

**9.** To join the four designs, pin the long edges of one 1¼" x 16" strip between the two design units, right sides together (Diagram C). Stitch.

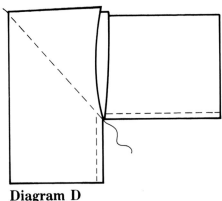

**Diagram C**

**10.** Mark the center of each side of the wall hanging and the centers of the long edges of the four remaining 16" light green sashing strips. With right sides together and centers matching, pin one strip to one side of the design unit. Stitch to within ¼" of each corner; backstitch. Repeat with the three remaining sashing strips.

**11.** To miter the corners, fold the right sides of two adjacent strips together and stitch at a 45° angle (Diagram D). Trim the seam allowance to ¼". Repeat for remaining corners.

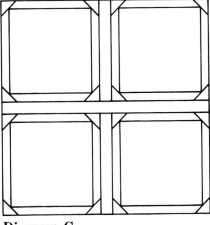

**Diagram D**

**12.** Mark the centers of the long edges of the dark green border strips. With right sides together and centers matching, pin border strips to two opposite sides of the wall hanging. Stitch.

**13.** With right sides together, stitch one 2¼" cinnamon square to each end of the two remaining border strips. With right sides together and centers matching, pin a border strip to each of the two remaining sides of the unit and stitch.

**14.** Pin the fleece to the wrong side of the pieced top. Then with right sides together, pin the top to the backing. Stitch, leaving a 6" opening on the top edge for turning. Trim the fleece from the seam allowances, clip the corners, and turn right side out. Slipstitch the opening closed.

**15.** Using white thread, quilt the edges of the design pieces by hand. Using dark green thread, quilt on both edges of all light green sashing pieces, stitching parallel to the seams. Quilt in the very center of the wall hanging to make a box with an X inside it. Quilt as close as possible to the long edge of each corner triangle.

**16.** With right sides together, fold the dark green pieces for the ties in half to measure 1¼" wide. Stitch along the 36" edges. Turn right side out. Turn the raw ends inside and slipstitch. Fold the ties in half to measure 1" x 18". Stitch the folds by hand to the back of the wall hanging near the top edge.

**Corner Triangle Pattern**

# DECEMBER 6
# *St. Nicholas Day*

When the Dutch settlers began migrating to America in the 1700s, they brought their St. Nicholas, or Sinter Klaas, with them. A bishop of the fourth century—tall, thin, and stately—the saint was known for caring for the needy. But in the New World, Sinter Klaas began to take on a new appearance—more like the newly arriving Dutch settlers. In Washington Irving's 1809 book on New York history, Sinter Klaas was depicted with a jolly red face and whiskers—and so the evolution of Santa began.

# *Sinter Klaas*

## SAMPLE
Stitched on white Belfast Linen 32 over two threads, the finished design size is 8¼" x 10¾". The fabric was cut 15" x 17".

| Anchor | | | DMC (used for sample) |
|---|---|---|---|

**Step 1:** Cross-stitch (two strands)

| | | | |
|---|---|---|---|
| 1 | ✓ | | White |
| 1 | R | | White (one strand) and Balger Metallic #032 Pearl (one strand) |
| 4146 | U | | 754 Peach Flesh-lt. |
| 868 | Z | | 758 Terra Cotta-lt. |
| 9 | S | | 760 Salmon |
| 46 | △ | | 321 Christmas Red |
| 47 | ✕ | | 304 Christmas Red-med. |
| 22 | ● | | 816 Garnet |

| | | | |
|---|---|---|---|
| 44 | B | | 814 Garnet-dk. |
| 128 | J | | 800 Delft-pale |
| 130 | N | | 809 Delft |
| 921 | K | | 931 Antique Blue-med. |
| 922 | ∴ | | 930 Antique Blue-dk. |
| 849 | ▢ | | 927 Slate Green-med. |
| 210 | H | | 562 Jade-med. |
| 876 | I | | 502 Blue Green |
| 878 | ▽ | | 501 Blue Green-dk. |
| 879 | ❖ | | 500 Blue Green-vy dk. |
| 885 | A | | 739 Tan-ultra vy. lt. |
| 942 | M | | 738 Tan-vy. lt. |
| 307 | + | | 977 Golden Brown-lt. |
| 324 | · | | 922 Copper-lt. |
| 339 | O | | 920 Copper-med. |
| 341 | + | | 918 Red Copper-dk. |
| 903 | ▲ | | 640 Beige Gray-vy. dk. |
| 378 | | | 841 Beige Brown-lt. |
| 379 | ▢ | | 840 Beige Brown-med. |
| 380 | ✕ | | 839 Beige Brown-dk. |
| 381 | E | | 838 Beige Brown-vy. dk. |
| 397 | G | | 762 Pearl Gray-vy. lt. |
| 398 | W | | 415 Pearl Gray |

**Step 2:** Filet Cross-stitch (one strand)

| | | | |
|---|---|---|---|
| 159 | O | | 827 Blue-vy. lt. |
| 920 | ■ | | 932 Antique Blue-lt. |
| 900 | · | | 928 Slate Green-lt. |
| 849 | − | | 927 Slate Green-med. |

**Step 3:** Backstitch (one strand)

| | | | |
|---|---|---|---|
| 46 | | | 321 Christmas Red (fringe, blanket) |
| 22 | | | 816 Garnet (lettering) |
| 922 | | | 930 Antique Blue-dk. (boy's pants, coat, gloves, hat, face) |
| 849 | | | 927 Slate Green-med. (border) |
| 379 | | | 840 Beige Brown-med. (puppy) |
| 400 | | | 317 Pewter Gray (beard, face) |
| 381 | | | 838 Beige Brown-vy. dk. (all else) |

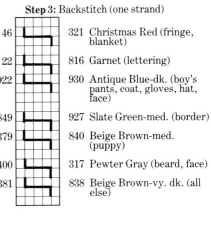

| FABRICS | DESIGN SIZES |
|---|---|
| Aida 11 | 11⅞" x 15¾" |
| Aida 14 | 9⅜" x 12⅜" |
| Aida 18 | 7¼" x 9⅝" |
| Hardanger 22 | 6" x 7⅞" |

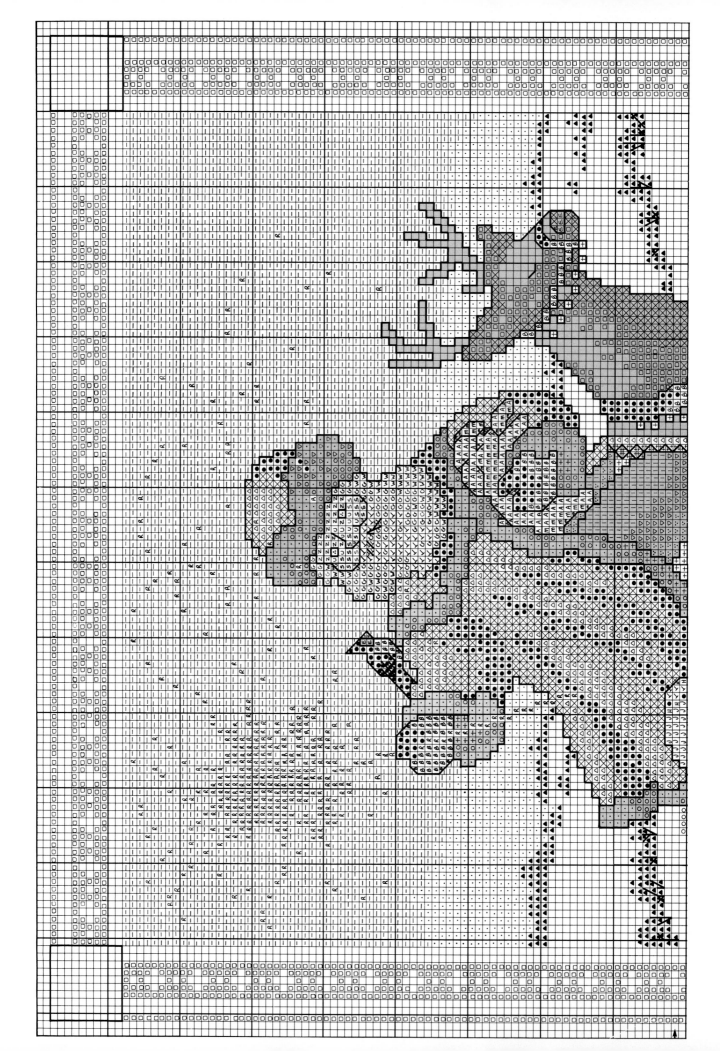

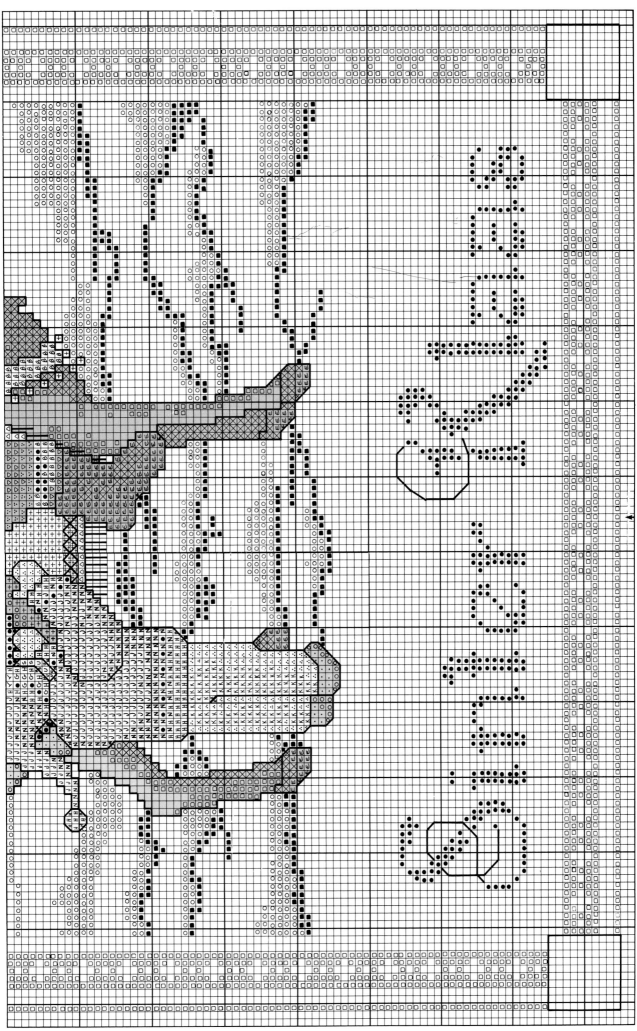

Stitch Count: 131 x 173

## DECEMBER 21

*First Day of Winter*

In our winter pillow, pastel pinks and blues create visions of dainty snowflakes dancing in the air, while a green and yellow center highlights the warmth of the holiday season. With this design we complete our Celebration of the Seasons set. So bring out the hot chocolate and relax with your pillows next to a glowing hearth.

# Winter Pillow

## SAMPLE
Stitched on white Belfast Linen 32 over two threads, the finished design size is 7″ x 7″. The fabric was cut 17″ x 17″. See Suppliers for information on ordering beads.

## MATERIALS
Completed cross-stitch on white Belfast Linen 32; matching thread
¾ yard of 45″-wide lightweight white satin
2 yards of purchased light pink bias tape; matching thread
Dressmakers' pen
14″ knife-edge pillow form

## DIRECTIONS
All seam allowances are ¼″.

1. With the design centered, cut a 13½″ square from the linen.

2. Cut one 13½″ square from satin for the pillow backing. Also cut four 5″ x 17″ bias strips for ruffles.

3. Draw a line down the lengthwise center of each strip. Place the raw edge of the bias tape next to the line, right sides together, and stitch ¼″ from the edge. Fold the tape back over the line and, keeping the tape smooth, topstitch it to the strip. Repeat with the remaining strips.

4. Fold one strip with right sides together to measure 2½″ wide; stitch the ends. Turn right side out. Press the strip with the fold in the center of the bias tape. Repeat with the three remaining strips.

5. Stitch a gathering thread close to the raw edges of one strip. Gather slightly to 13″; repeat for remaining strips to make four ruffles. Place the ruffles on the pillow top with right sides together, raw edges aligned, and the ends of ruffles ¼″ from the pillow corners. Baste in place.

6. Place the pillow back and top, right sides together, with ruffles tucked between them. Stitch, leaving a 5″ opening for turning. Clip the corners and turn right side out. Insert pillow form. Slipstitch the opening closed.

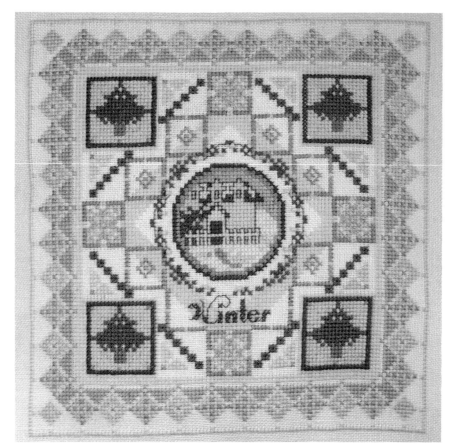

**Stitch Count: 112 x 112**

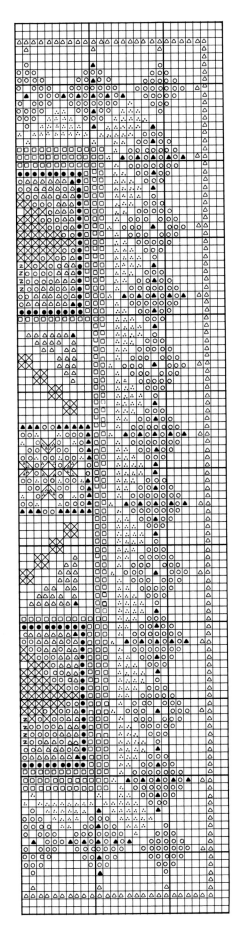

| Anchor | | DMC (used for sample) |
|---|---|---|

**Step 1:** Cross-stitch (two strands)

| Anchor | | DMC | |
|---|---|---|---|
| 1 | • | | White |
| 295 | E | 726 | Topaz-lt. |
| 306 | + | 725 | Topaz |
| 892 | △ | 225 | Shell Pink-vy. lt. |
| 69 | N | 3687 | Mauve |
| 158 | O | 747 | Sky Blue-vy. lt. |
| 159 | ∴ / | 827 | Blue-vy. lt. |
| 167 | ▲ | 519 | Sky Blue |
| 978 | ● / | 322 | Navy Blue-vy. lt. |
| 187 | X | 992 | Aquamarine |
| 378 | Z | 841 | Beige Brown-lt. |
| 379 | ■ | 840 | Beige Brown-med. |
| 398 | H | 415 | Pearl Gray |

**Step 2:** Filet Cross-stitch (one strand)

| Anchor | | DMC | |
|---|---|---|---|
| 886 | − / | 677 | Old Gold-vy. lt. |
| 885 | □ | 739 | Tan-ultra vy. lt. |

**Step 3:** Backstitch (one strand)

| Anchor | | DMC | |
|---|---|---|---|
| 978 | | 322 | Navy Blue-vy. lt. (lettering) |
| 187 | | 992 | Aquamarine (wreath around center design) |
| 379 | | 840 | Beige Brown-med. (house, fence) |

**Step 4:** Beadwork

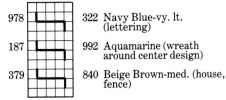

Pink (MPR 145T)

**FABRICS**
Aida 11
Aida 14
Aida 18
Hardanger 22

**DESIGN SIZES**
10⅛" x 10⅛"
8" x 8"
6¼" x 6¼"
5⅛" x 5⅛"

## DECEMBER 25
# Christmas

Shepherds and Wise Men jour-
neyed to Bethlehem nearly two
thousand years ago to celebrate
the birth of Christ. Eager to find
this newborn king, they pro-
claimed His birth with songs of
praise and precious gifts. Today,
as we recall that first Christmas
so very long ago, we still joyously
sing the songs and share the gifts
of the Yuletide season.

# Yuletide
# Stockings

**SAMPLES**
**Wise Men Stocking:** Stitched on
white Hardanger 22 over two
threads, the finished design size is
10¼″ x 15¼″. The fabric was cut
14″ x 18″.

**Shepherds Stocking:** Stitched on
white Hardanger 22 over two
threads, finished design size is 10″
x 15⅛″. Fabric was cut 14″ x 18″.

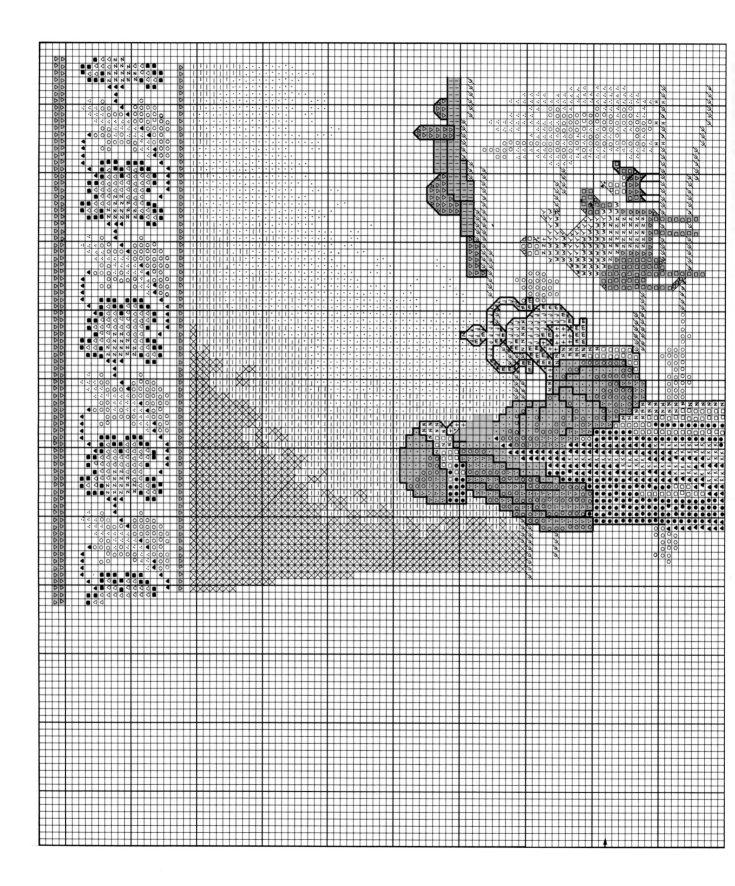

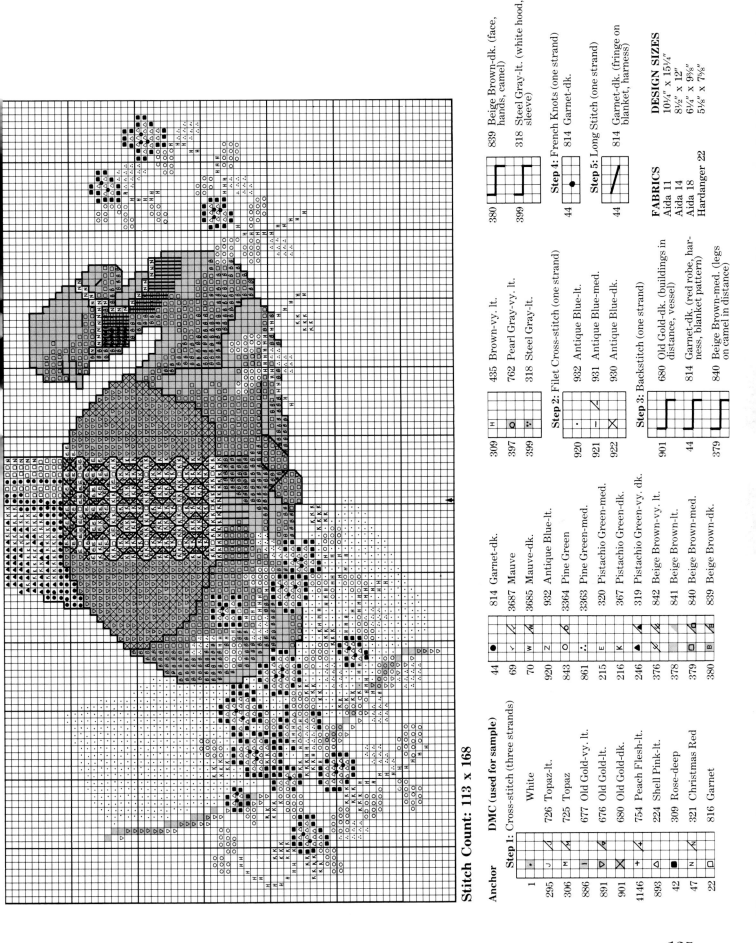

**Stitch Count: 113 x 168**

| Anchor | | DMC (used for sample) |
|---|---|---|
| | | **Step 1:** Cross-stitch (three strands) |
| 1 | · | White |
| 295 | J | 726 Topaz-lt. |
| 306 | M | 725 Topaz |
| 886 | 1 | 677 Old Gold-vy. lt. |
| 891 | ▷ | 676 Old Gold-lt. |
| 901 | X | 680 Old Gold-dk. |
| 1146 | + | 754 Peach Flesh-lt. |
| 893 | ◁ | 224 Shell Pink-lt. |
| 42 | ■ | 309 Rose-deep |
| 47 | N | 321 Christmas Red |
| 22 | ▭ | 816 Garnet |

| | | |
|---|---|---|
| 44 | ● | 814 Garnet-dk. |
| 69 | ⟍ | 3687 Mauve |
| 70 | ⟍ | 3685 Mauve-dk. |
| 920 | Z | 932 Antique Blue-lt. |
| 843 | O | 3364 Pine Green |
| 861 | ∴ | 3363 Pine Green-med. |
| 215 | E | 320 Pistachio Green-med. |
| 216 | K | 367 Pistachio Green-dk. |
| 246 | ◀ | 319 Pistachio Green-vy. dk. |
| 376 | ⟋ | 842 Beige Brown-vy. lt. |
| 378 | | 841 Beige Brown-lt. |
| 379 | ◻ | 840 Beige Brown-med. |
| 380 | B | 839 Beige Brown-dk. |

| | | |
|---|---|---|
| 309 | H | 435 Brown-vy. lt. |
| 397 | O | 762 Pearl Gray-vy. lt. |
| 399 | ∴ | 318 Steel Gray-lt. |
| | | **Step 2:** Filet Cross-stitch (one strand) |
| 920 | · | 932 Antique Blue-lt. |
| 921 | — | 931 Antique Blue-med. |
| 922 | X | 930 Antique Blue-dk. |
| | | **Step 3:** Backstitch (one strand) |
| 901 | | 680 Old Gold-dk. (buildings in distance, vessel) |
| 44 | | 814 Garnet-dk. (red robe, harness, blanket pattern) |
| 379 | | 840 Beige Brown-med. (legs on camel in distance) |

| | | |
|---|---|---|
| 380 | | 839 Beige Brown-dk. (face, hands, camel) |
| 399 | | 318 Steel Gray-lt. (white hood, sleeve) |
| | | **Step 4:** French Knots (one strand) |
| 44 | ● | 814 Garnet-dk. |
| | | **Step 5:** Long Stitch (one strand) |
| 44 | | 814 Garnet-dk. (fringe on blanket, harness) |

**FABRICS**   **DESIGN SIZES**
Aida 11   10¼" x 15¼"
Aida 14   8½" x 12"
Aida 18   6¼" x 9⅜"
Hardanger 22   5⅛" x 7⅞"

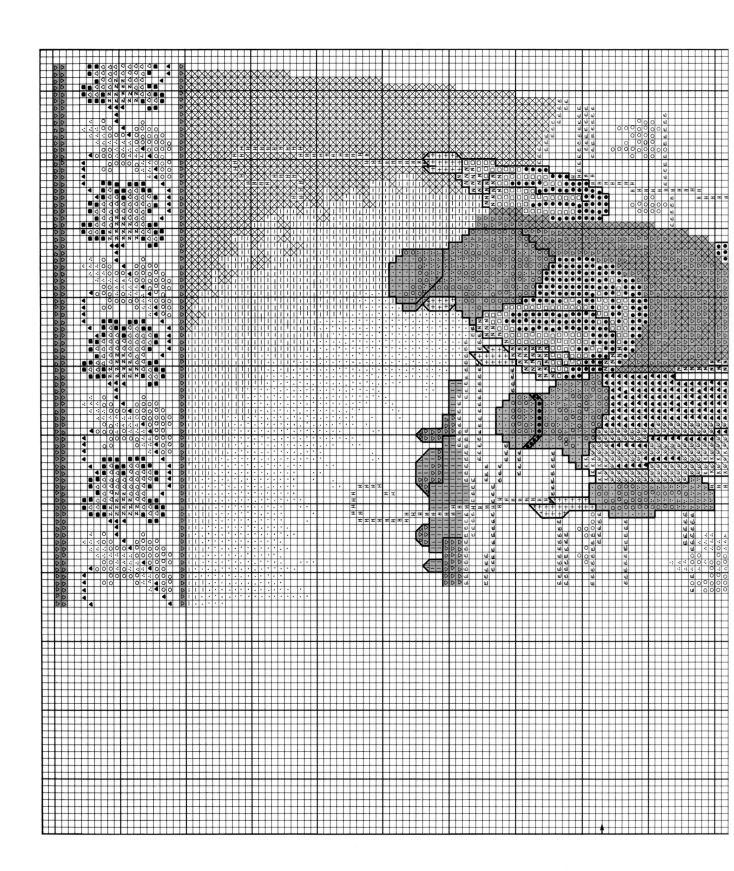

126

**Stitch Count: 110 x 166**

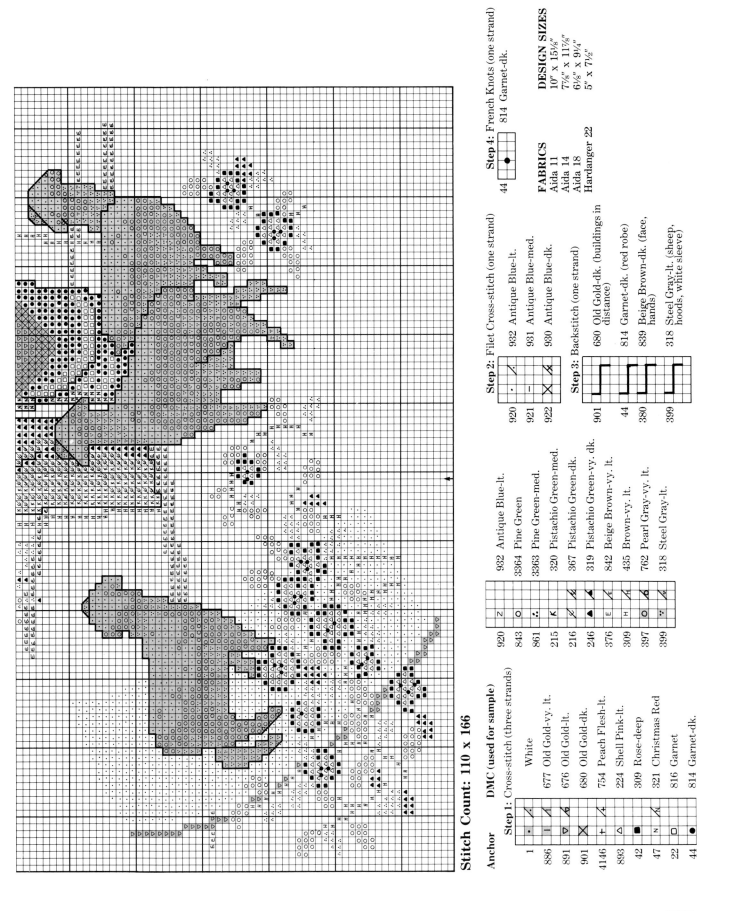

**MATERIALS (for one stocking)**
Completed cross-stitch on white
 Hardanger 22
¾ yard of 45″-wide blue faille
 fabric; matching thread
1¼ yards of small cording
½ yard of flannel
⅛ yard of 45″-wide metallic gold
 fabric
Metallic gold thread
1½ yards of ⅜″-wide blue pleated
 ribbon
1 yard of ⅜″-wide blue picot-
 edged satin ribbon
2 yards of ¼″-wide gold metallic
 ribbon
Paper for pattern
Dressmakers' pen
Large-eyed needle for couching

**Stocking Pattern**
(Add ¼″ seam allowance.)

## DIRECTIONS
All seam allowances are ¼″.

1. Make pattern for stocking.

2. For the stocking front, align the top edge of the pattern with the top edge of the stitched design. (Portions of the stitched design will extend into the seam allowance.) Add ¼″ seam allowances as you cut the stocking.

3. From the blue fabric, cut one stocking piece for the backing and two stocking pieces for the lining. Cut 1″-wide bias strips, piecing as needed, to measure 1¼ yards. Cover the cording, leaving it somewhat loose in the casing.

4. Cut two stocking pieces from flannel for the inner lining.

5. From gold fabric, cut one 2½″ x 24½″ strip for the ruffle. With right sides together, fold the strip in half lengthwise and then stitch the 1¼″ ends. Turn right side out. Pin ¼″-deep pleats 1″ apart in the ruffle (Diagram A). The pleated strip should measure 14″; adjust pleats if necessary.

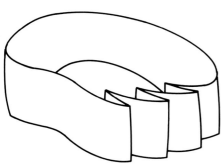

**Diagram A**

6. With raw edges aligned, sew the cording all around the right side of the stocking front (except the top edge), using the stitching line on the cording as a sewing guide.

7. Pin the flannel stocking pieces to the wrong sides of the stocking front and back. Then, with right sides together, sew the front to the back, sewing on the stitching line of the cording. Be sure to catch the flannel in the seam. Clip the curved seams. Turn right side out.

8. Pin the pleated strip around the top edge of the stocking, aligning raw edges (Diagram B).

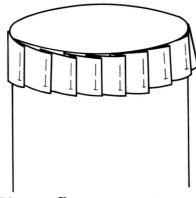

**Diagram B**

9. With right sides together, sew the lining pieces to one another. Clip the curved seams. Do not turn right side out. Slide the lining over the stocking, right sides together and side seams matching. Stitch around the top of the stocking, leaving an opening for turning. Turn the stocking through the opening and slide the lining inside the stocking. Slipstitch the opening closed.

10. Thread needle with one strand of metallic thread and wrap thread around cording at ¼″ intervals, angling your stitch (Diagram C).

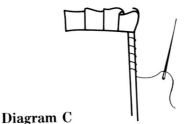

**Diagram C**

11. Fold the pleated ribbon into one 8″ loop and one 5″ loop, leaving 12″ ends; pin to secure and set aside. Fold the picot ribbon into one 6″ loop and one 2″ loop, leaving 9″ ends; pin. Cut one 6″ and one 24″ length of gold ribbon; set aside. From the remaining gold ribbon, fold two 4″ loops, leaving 12″ ends; pin. Align the centers of all loops. Tie the 24″ length of gold ribbon in a bow around the centers; knot. Tack the knot to the upper right corner of the stocking front.

12. For the hanger, fold the 6″ length of gold ribbon in half and tack the ends inside the right-hand seam of the stocking.

| Anchor | | | DMC (used for sample) | |
|---|---|---|---|---|
| | | | **Step 1:** Cross-stitch (two strands) | |
| 1 | · | ⁄ | | White |
| 306 | S | ⁄ | 725 | Topaz |
| 868 | ∴ | ⁄ | 758 | Terra Cotta-lt. |
| 5975 | H | | 356 | Terra Cotta-med. |
| 869 | ✕ | | 3042 | Antique Violet-lt. |
| 871 | ● | ⁄ | 3041 | Antique Violet-med. |
| 970 | E | E | 315 | Antique Mauve-dk. |
| 158 | □ | | 828 | Blue-ultra lt. |
| 887 | ▽ | ⁄ | 372 | Mustard-lt. |
| 859 | O | ⁄ | 522 | Fern Green |
| 885 | + | ⁄ | 739 | Tan-ultra lt. |
| 942 | ✕ | | 738 | Tan-vy. lt. |
| 362 | ▲ | | 437 | Tan-lt. |
| 376 | I | ⁄ | 842 | Beige Brown-vy. lt. |
| 378 | O | ⁄ | 841 | Beige Brown-lt. |
| 379 | ● | ⁄ | 840 | Beige Brown-med. |
| 388 | + | ⁄ | 3033 | Mocha Brown-vy. lt. |
| 933 | · | | 543 | Beige Brown-ultra lt. |
| 8581 | ∴ | ⁄ | 3023 | Brown Gray-lt. |
| 397 | R | R | 3072 | Beaver Gray-vy. lt. |
| 397 | △ | ⁄ | 453 | Shell Gray-lt. |

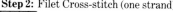

**Step 2:** Filet Cross-stitch (one strand)

| Anchor | | DMC |
|---|---|---|
| 158 | | 828 Blue-ultra lt. |
| 920 | − | 932 Antique Blue-lt. |

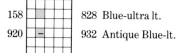

**Step 3:** Backstitch (one strand)

| Anchor | | DMC |
|---|---|---|
| 5975 | | 356 Terra Cotta-med. (reins) |
| 920 | | 932 Antique Blue-lt. (doves, wise men, sand) |
| 921 | | 931 Antique Blue-med. (all else) |

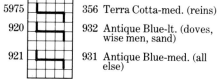

**Step 4:** French Knots (one strand)

| Anchor | | DMC |
|---|---|---|
| 921 | ● | 931 Antique Blue-med. |

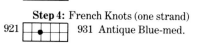

**Step 5:** Long Stitch (one strand)

| Anchor | | DMC |
|---|---|---|
| 306 | ╱ | 725 Topaz (star) |

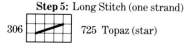

# Wise Men Still Seek Him

**SAMPLE**

Stitched on white Belfast Linen 32 over two threads, the finished design size is 6″ x 8″. The fabric was cut 12″ x 14″.

| FABRICS | DESIGN SIZES |
|---|---|
| Aida 11 | 8¾″ x 11⅝″ |
| Aida 14 | 6⅞″ x 9⅛″ |
| Aida 18 | 5⅜″ x 7⅛″ |
| Hardanger 22 | 4⅜″ x 5⅞″ |

**Stitch Count: 96 x 128**

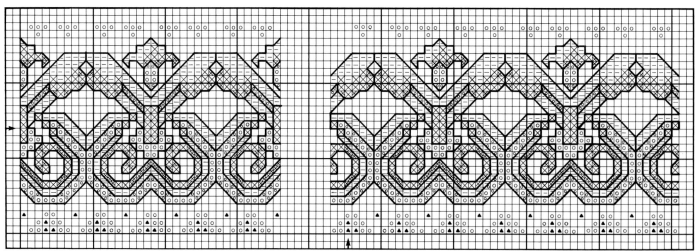

**Right Green Towel Stitch Counts: 36 x 28 (left section)**     48 x 28 (center section)

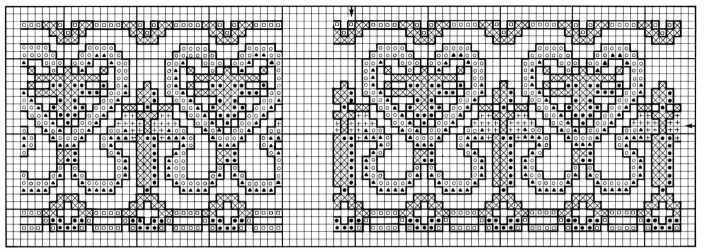

**Center Green Towel Stitch Counts: 36 x 28 (left section)**     **48 x 28 (center section)**

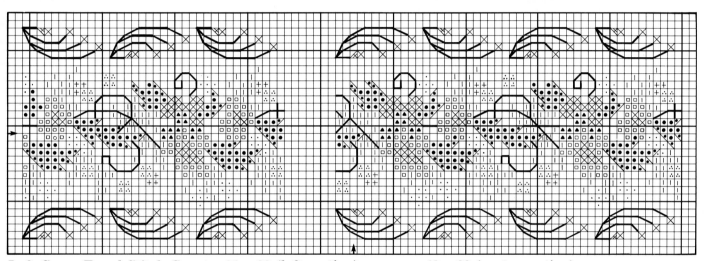

**Left Green Towel Stitch Counts: 36 x 28 (left section)**     **48 x 28 (center section)**

# *Towels*

## SAMPLES

**Right Green Towel:** Design was stitched on a deep teal Fingertip Towel 14. Repeat left section of graph on right section of towel.

| Anchor | | | DMC (used for sample) |
|---|---|---|---|
| | | **Step 1:** Cross-stitch (two strands) | |
| 891 | – | ⁄ | 676 Old Gold-lt. |
| 890 | X | ⁄ | 729 Old Gold-med. |
| 47 | O | ⁄ | 304 Christmas Red-med. |
| 22 | ▲ | | 816 Garnet |

**Step 2:** Backstitch (one strand)

Metallic Gold Madeira
Super Twist #30

**Center Green Towel:** The design was stitched on a deep teal Christmas Fingertip Towel 14. Repeat the left section of the graph on the right section of the towel.

| Anchor | | DMC (used for sample) |
|---|---|---|
| | **Step 1:** Cross-stitch (two strands) | |
| 890 | X | 729 Old Gold-med. |
| 901 | ● | 680 Old Gold-dk. |
| 47 | + | 321 Christmas Red |
| 20 | O | 498 Christmas Red-dk. |
| 43 | ▲ | 815 Garnet-med. |
| 216 | ▢ | 367 Pistachio Green-dk. |

**Step 2:** Backstitch (one strand)

Gold Metallic Madeira
Super Twist #30

**Left Green Towel:** The design was stitched on a deep teal Christmas Fingertip Towel 14. Repeat the left section of the graph on the right section of the towel.

| Anchor | | | DMC (used for sample) |
|---|---|---|---|
| | | **Step 1:** Cross-stitch (two strands) | |
| 891 | · | ⁄ | 676 Old Gold-lt. |
| 11 | ▢ | | 351 Coral |
| 13 | X | ⁄ | 349 Coral-dk. |
| 44 | ▲ | | 816 Garnet |
| 869 | ⁖ | | 3042 Antique Violet-lt. |
| 871 | + | | 3041 Antique Violet-med. |
| 875 | I | ⁄ | 503 Blue Green-med. |
| 244 | ● | ⁄ | 987 Forest Green-dk. |

**Step 2:** Backstitch (one strand)

| 244 | | 987 Forest Green-dk. |
|---|---|---|

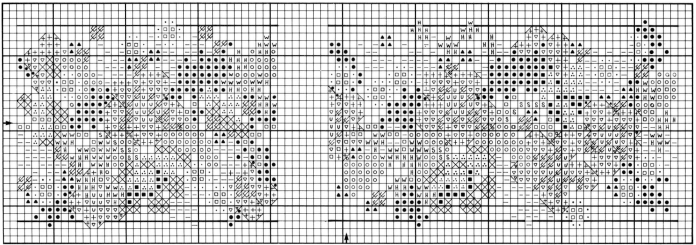

**Lower Red Towel Stitch Counts: 36 x 28 (left section)**     **48 x 28 (center section)**

**Lower Red Towel:** The design was stitched on a rich cranberry Christmas Fingertip Towel 14. Repeat the left section of the graph on the right section of the towel.

| Anchor | | DMC (used for sample) |
|---|---|---|
| **Step 1:** Cross-stitch (two strands) | | |
| 886 | | 677 Old Gold-vy. lt. |
| 890 | U | 729 Old Gold-med. |
| 11 | + | 351 Coral |
| 13 | ▽ | 349 Coral-dk. |
| 22 | ✕ | 816 Garnet |

| 44 | ▲ | 814 Garnet-dk. |
|---|---|---|
| 869 | ∴ | 3042 Antique Violet-lt. |
| 871 | ✕ | 3041 Antique Violet-med. |
| 101 | ■ | 327 Antique Violet-dk. |
| 900 | W | 928 Slate Green-lt. |
| 849 | H | 927 Slate Green-med. |
| 875 | — | 503 Blue Green-med. |

| 243 | O | 988 Forest Green-med. |
|---|---|---|
| 244 | S | 987 Forest Green-dk. |
| 879 | ● | 890 Pistachio Green-ultra dk. |
| 363 | ▢ | 436 Tan |

**Step 2:** Backstitch (one strand)

| 879 | | 890 Pistachio Green-ultra dk. |
|---|---|---|

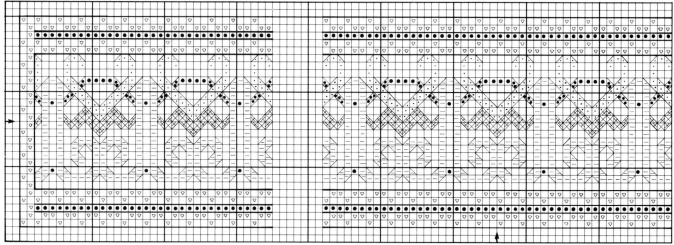

**Right Red Towel Stitch Count: 132 x 28 (entire design)**

**Right Red Towel:** The design was stitched on a rich cranberry Christmas Fingertip Towel 14.

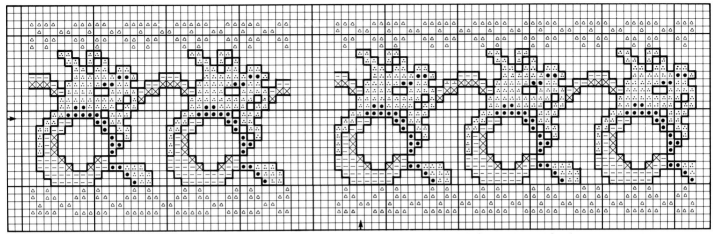

**Upper Red Towel Stitch Counts: 36 x 26 (left section)    50 x 26 (center section)**

**Upper Red Towel:** The design was stitched on a rich cranberry Christmas Fingertip Towel 14. Repeat the left section of the graph on the right section of the towel.

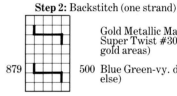

| Anchor | | DMC (used for sample) |
|---|---|---|
| | **Step 1:** Cross-stitch (two strands) | |
| 891 | − | 676 Old Gold-lt. |
| 901 | ✕ | 680 Old Gold-dk. |

| 216 | ∴ | 367 Pistachio Green-dk. |
|---|---|---|
| 878 | • | 501 Blue Green-dk. |
| | △ | Gold Metallic Madeira Super Twist #30 (one strand) |

**Step 2:** Backstitch (one strand)

Gold Metallic Madeira Super Twist #30 (around gold areas)

| 879 | | 500 Blue Green-vy. dk. (all else) |
|---|---|---|

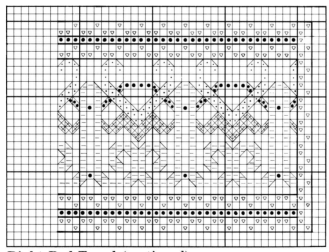

**Right Red Towel** (continued)

| Anchor | | DMC (used for sample) |
|---|---|---|
| | **Step 1:** Cross-stitch (two strands) | |
| 886 | • ⁄ | 677 Old Gold-vy. lt. |
| 891 | − ⁄ | 676 Old Gold-lt. |
| 890 | ✕ ⁄ | 729 Old Gold-med. |

| 878 | ● ⁄ | 501 Blue Green-dk. (one strand) and Metallic Green Madeira Super Twist #30 (one strand) |
|---|---|---|
| | ◿ | Metallic Gold Madeira Super Twist #30 |

**Step 2:** Backstitch (one strand)

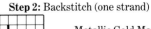

Metallic Gold Madeira Super Twist #30

# Victorian Stocking

Stitched on baby pink Linda 27 over two threads, the finished design size is 3¾" x 6⅝". The fabric was cut 6" x 9".

**MATERIALS**
Completed cross-stitch on baby pink Linda 27
5" x 8" piece of unstitched baby pink Linda 27; matching thread
Two 6" x 8" pieces of pink/white check fabric for lining
1 yard of ⅛"-wide light green satin ribbon; matching thread
Trinkets
8" x 11½" mat board
Glue
Tracing paper for pattern
Dressmakers' pen

**DIRECTIONS**
All seam allowances are ¼".

**1.** Trace and cut out the stocking pattern. Place on the Linda with design centered. Cut one stocking from unstitched Linda for back.

**2.** Cut two stocking pieces from the lining fabric.

**3.** With right sides together, stitch Linda front to back. Clip curves. Turn right side out.

**4.** With right sides together, sew the two lining pieces together.

**5.** Slide the lining, wrong side out, over the stocking, matching the side seams. Stitch around the top, leaving a 3" opening, and turn right side out. Slide the lining down into the stocking and slip-stitch the opening closed.

**6.** Cut ribbon into two equal lengths and handle as one. Tie a bow with 1½" loops. Tack the bow to the stocking (see photo).

**7.** Position the stocking on the mat board and glue in place. Glue the trinkets in place as desired. Frame the mat board in a shadow box that is at least 1" deep.

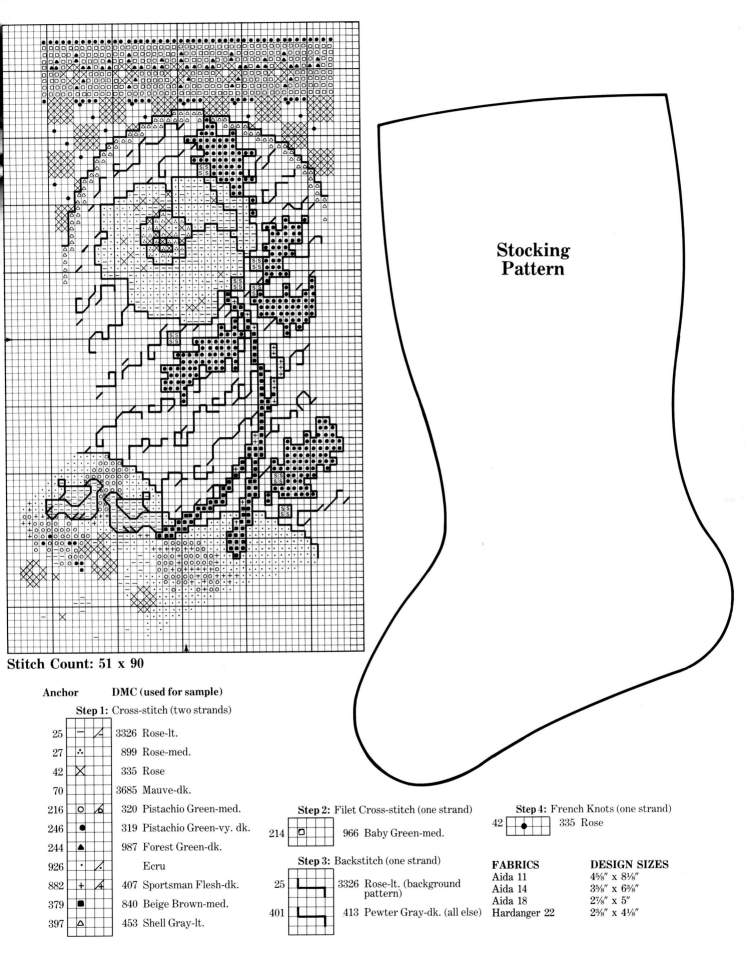

**Stocking Pattern**

**Stitch Count: 51 x 90**

| Anchor | | | DMC (used for sample) |
|---|---|---|---|

**Step 1:** Cross-stitch (two strands)

| Anchor | | | DMC |
|---|---|---|---|
| 25 | — | ╱ | 3326 Rose-lt. |
| 27 | ∴ | | 899 Rose-med. |
| 42 | ✕ | | 335 Rose |
| 70 | | | 3685 Mauve-dk. |
| 216 | ○ | ◢ | 320 Pistachio Green-med. |
| 246 | ● | | 319 Pistachio Green-vy. dk. |
| 244 | ▲ | | 987 Forest Green-dk. |
| 926 | · | ╱ | Ecru |
| 882 | + | ◢ | 407 Sportsman Flesh-dk. |
| 379 | ■ | | 840 Beige Brown-med. |
| 397 | △ | | 453 Shell Gray-lt. |

**Step 2:** Filet Cross-stitch (one strand)

| | | |
|---|---|---|
| 214 | ▫ | 966 Baby Green-med. |

**Step 3:** Backstitch (one strand)

| | | |
|---|---|---|
| 25 | | 3326 Rose-lt. (background pattern) |
| 401 | | 413 Pewter Gray-dk. (all else) |

**Step 4:** French Knots (one strand)

| | | |
|---|---|---|
| 42 | ● | 335 Rose |

| FABRICS | DESIGN SIZES |
|---|---|
| Aida 11 | 4⅝" x 8⅛" |
| Aida 14 | 3⅝" x 6⅜" |
| Aida 18 | 2⅞" x 5" |
| Hardanger 22 | 2⅜" x 4⅛" |

## DECEMBER 31
# New Year's Eve

Ring out the old! Ring in the new! Tonight bubbly party-goers will toast the new year amid the ping of champagne glasses, noisemakers, confetti, and streamers. Masked balls are a New Year's Eve tradition in many areas, and these cross-stitched masks will add that extra sparkle to your revelry.

# Holiday Masks

**SAMPLES**

**Gold Mask:** Stitched on cream Belfast Linen 32 over two threads, the finished design size is 7½" x 3¾". The fabric was cut 12" x 8".

**Lavender Mask:** Stitched on white Belfast Linen 32 over two threads, the finished design size is 7½" x 4⅛". The fabric was cut 12" x 8". See Suppliers for information on ordering beads.

**MATERIALS (for one mask)**
Completed cross-stitch on cream or white Belfast Linen 32; matching thread
One 9½" x 5½" piece of un-stitched Belfast Linen 32
Two 9½" x 5½" pieces of fusible interfacing
1 yard of 24-gauge covered wire

Dressmakers' pen
Tracing paper for patterns
Glue

**For Lavender Mask:**
One 15"-long, ¼"-wide dowel
Lavender paint
3 yards of ⅛"-wide lavender satin ribbon

3 yards of 1/16"-wide light lavender satin ribbon
3 yards of 1/16"-wide pink satin ribbon
3 yards of 1/16"-wide dark green rayon ribbon

**For Gold Mask:**
Two 5"-6" white feathers

## DIRECTIONS

**1.** Trace and cut out the mask pattern. Place the pattern on the wrong side of stitched design, checking placement against stitching. Trace the outline with the dressmakers' pen. Also trace onto the unstitched linen. Cut both pieces ¼″ outside pen line.

**2.** Fuse one piece of interfacing to the wrong side of the design and one piece to the wrong side of the unstitched linen. Trim interfacing on both pieces to match linen.

**3.** Place the design piece and the unstitched piece with right sides together. Stitch on the pen line, using a small stitch and pivoting at the scallops. Leave a small opening for turning. Trim all seam allowances to ⅛″. Turn right side out and slipstitch the opening closed. Press carefully.

**4.** Trace the openings for the eyes on the right side of the design piece. Machine-satin-stitch on the pen line through all layers. Cut out the openings for the eyes. Then stitch the beads to mask; see the graph for placement.

**5.** Slipstitch the wire around the back of the mask, ¼″ from the outside edge, following the general shape of the mask. Add a second length of wire between the eye openings and the top edge for more shaping control.

**6. Lavender Mask:** Paint the dowel. Glue it to the back right-hand edge of the mask. Cut all ribbons in half. Handling the ribbon lengths as one, tie into a 6″ bow with streamers. Tack to the edge of the mask near the dowel.

**7. Gold Mask:** Glue two feathers to the front of the mask near the left edge.

**Stitch Count: 120 x 66**

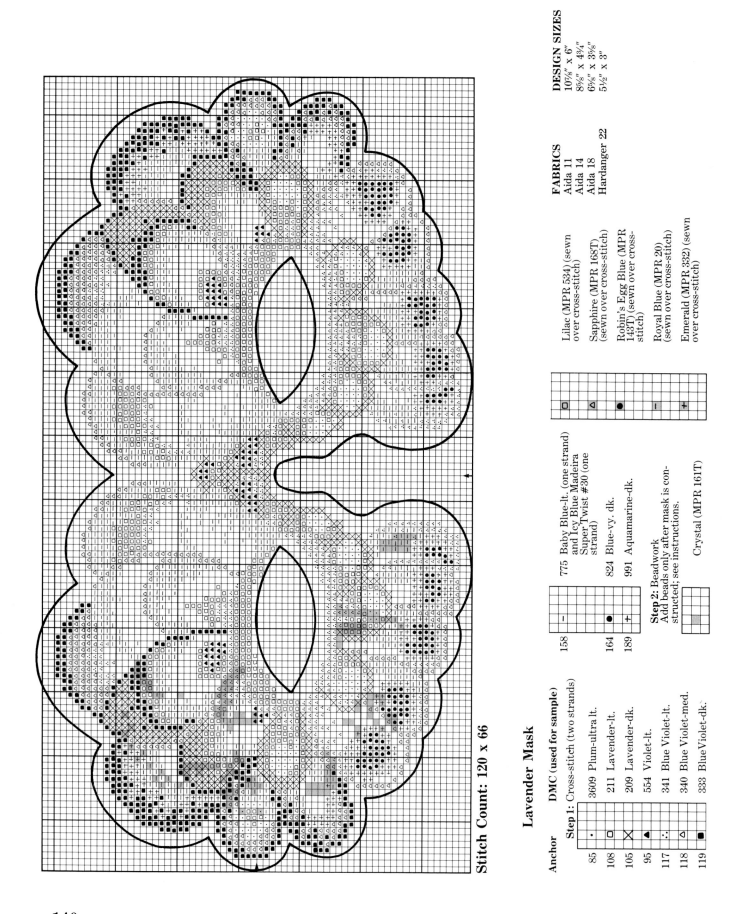

## Lavender Mask

| Anchor | DMC (used for sample) |
|---|---|

**Step 1:** Cross-stitch (two strands)

| | | Anchor | | |
|---|---|---|---|---|
| • | | 85 | | 3609 Plum-ultra lt. |
| □ | | 108 | | 211 Lavender-lt. |
| ✕ | | 105 | | 209 Lavender-dk. |
| ◢ | | 95 | | 554 Violet-lt. |
| ∴ | | 117 | | 341 Blue Violet-lt. |
| ◿ | | 118 | | 340 Blue Violet-med. |
| ■ | | 119 | | 333 Blue Violet-dk. |

| | | | |
|---|---|---|---|
| − | | 158 | 775 Baby Blue-lt. (one strand) and Icy Blue Madeira Super Twist #30 (one strand) |
| ● | | 164 | 824 Blue-vy. dk. |
| + | | 189 | 991 Aquamarine-dk. |

**Step 2:** Beadwork

Add beads only after mask is constructed; see instructions.

Crystal (MPR 161T)

**DESIGN SIZES**

| FABRICS | |
|---|---|
| Aida 11 | 10⅞" x 6" |
| Aida 14 | 8⅝" x 4¾" |
| Aida 18 | 6⅝" x 3⅝" |
| Hardanger 22 | 5½" x 3" |

Lilac (MPR 534) (sewn over cross-stitch)

Sapphire (MPR 168T) (sewn over cross-stitch)

Robin's Egg Blue (MPR 143T) (sewn over cross-stitch)

Royal Blue (MPR 20)

Emerald (MPR 332) (sewn over cross-stitch)

| □ | | ◿ | | ● | | I | | + |
|---|---|---|---|---|---|---|---|---|

**Stitch Count: 119 x 60**

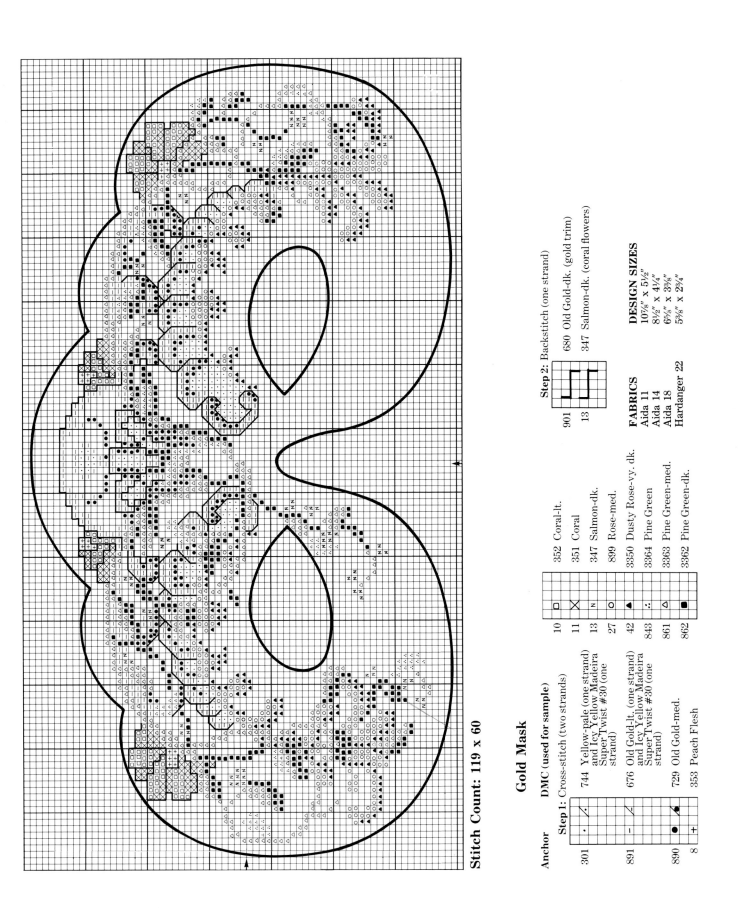

## Gold Mask

**Anchor**   **DMC (used for sample)**

**Step 1:** Cross-stitch (two strands)

| Anchor | | | DMC |
|---|---|---|---|
| 301 | · | ⁄ | 744 Yellow-pale (one strand) and Icy Yellow Madeira Super Twist #30 (one strand) |
| 891 | − | ⁄ | 676 Old Gold-lt. (one strand) and Icy Yellow Madeira Super Twist #30 (one strand) |
| 890 | ● | ◀ | 729 Old Gold-med. |
| 8 | + | | 353 Peach Flesh |

| | | DMC |
|---|---|---|
| 10 | □ | 352 Coral-lt. |
| 11 | X | 351 Coral |
| 13 | N | 347 Salmon-dk. |
| 27 | O | 899 Rose-med. |
| 42 | ◀ | 3350 Dusty Rose-vy. dk. |
| 843 | ∴ | 3364 Pine Green |
| 861 | △ | 3363 Pine Green-med. |
| 862 | ■ | 3362 Pine Green-dk. |

**Step 2:** Backstitch (one strand)

| 901 | | 680 Old Gold-dk. (gold trim) |
|---|---|---|
| 13 | | 347 Salmon-dk. (coral flowers) |

**DESIGN SIZES**

**FABRICS**
Aida 11   10⅞" x 5½"
Aida 14   8½" x 4¼"
Aida 18   6⅝" x 3⅜"
Hardanger 22   5⅜" x 2¾"

# General Instructions

## CROSS-STITCH

**Fabrics:** Most fabrics used in this book are even-weave fabrics made especially for cross-stitch and are available in needlework departments or shops. If you cannot find the fabrics in your area, refer to Suppliers. Fabrics used for the models in the photographs are identified in the sample information by color, name, and thread count per inch.

**Finished Design Size:** To determine the finished size of a design, divide the stitch count by the threads per inch of the fabric. When designs are stitched over two threads, divide stitch count by half of the threads per inch.

**Needles:** Use a blunt tapestry needle that slips easily through the holes and does not pierce the fabric. With fabric that has eleven or fewer threads per inch, use needle size 24; with fourteen threads per inch, use needle size 24 or 26; with eighteen threads or more per inch, use needle size 26.

**Preparing Fabric:** Cut the fabric 3″ larger on all sides than the finished design size, or cut as indicated in sample information. To keep the fabric from fraying, whipstitch or machine-zigzag the raw edges.

**Hoop or Frame:** Select a hoop or stretcher bars large enough to hold the entire design. Place the screw or clamp of the hoop in a 10 o'clock position (or 2 o'clock, if you are left-handed) to keep from catching the thread.

**Floss:** Cut the floss into 18″ lengths. For best coverage, run the floss over a damp sponge and separate all six strands. Put back together the number of strands recommended for use in sample information. If the floss becomes twisted while stitching, drop the needle and allow the floss to unwind. The floss will cover best when lying flat.

**Centering Design:** Find the center of the fabric by folding it from top to bottom and again from left to right. Place a pin in the point of the fold to mark the center. Locate the center of the graph by following the vertical and horizontal arrows. Begin stitching at the center point of the graph and fabric. Each square on the graph represents a complete cross-stitch. Unless indicated otherwise in the sample information, each stitch is over one unit of thread.

**Securing Floss:** Never knot floss unless working on clothing. Hold 1″ of thread behind fabric and secure the thread with the first few stitches. To secure the thread when finishing, run it under four or more stitches on the back of the design.

**Backstitching:** Complete all cross-stitches before working backstitches or accent stitches. When backstitching, use the number of strands indicated in the code or one strand fewer than was used for cross-stitching.

**Stitching Method:** For a smooth stitch, use a "push and pull" method. Push the needle straight down and completely through the fabric before pulling it up.

**Carrying Floss:** Do not carry floss more than ½″ between stitched areas because the loose threads, especially dark ones, will show through the fabric. Run the floss under worked stitches on back when possible.

**Cleaning Completed Work:** After making sure fabric and floss are colorfast, briefly soak the completed work in cold water. If it is soiled, wash it gently in mild soap. Roll the work in a towel to remove excess water; do not wring. Place the work face down on a dry lightweight towel and press it with a warm iron until it is dry.

## STITCHES

**Cross-Stitch:** Bring the needle and thread up at A, down at B, up at C, and down again at D (Diagram A). For rows, stitch all the way across so that the floss is angled from the lower left to the upper right; then return (Diagram B). *All the stitches should lie in the same direction.*

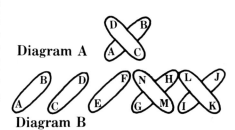

Diagram A

Diagram B

**Half-Cross:** Indicated on the graph by a slanted line with the color symbol beside it; make the longer stitch in the direction of the slanted line. The half-cross stitch actually fits three-fourths of the area (Diagram C).

Diagram C

Bring the needle and thread up at A and down at B, up at C and down at D. In cases where the two colors meet, the graph will indicate how the colors make up the completed stitch (Diagram D).

**Diagram D**

**Filet Cross-Stitch:** Filet cross-stitch is simply cross-stitch that uses only one strand of embroidery floss. It is usually used for the background of a design, while the design itself is cross-stitched with enough strands to cover the fabric. When complete, the background resembles a delicate net (see St. Nicholas Day).

**Backstitch:** Work from left to right with one strand of floss (unless indicated otherwise in the code). Bring needle and thread up at A, down at B, and up again at C. Going back down again at A, continue in this manner (Diagram E).

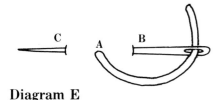

**Diagram E**

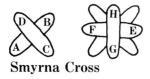

**Smyrna Cross**

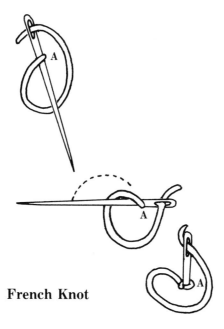

**French Knot**

## BEADWORK
With one strand of embroidery floss, attach beads to fabric with a half-cross, lower left to upper right. Secure the beads by returning the thread through the beads, lower right to upper left. Complete an entire row of half-crosses before returning to secure all the beads. See Suppliers for the source of beads used for the projects throughout the book.

## WORKING WITH WASTE CANVAS
Cut the waste canvas 1″ larger on all sides than the finished design size. Baste the waste canvas to the fabric or paper to be stitched. Complete the stitching; each stitch is over one unit (two threads). When stitching is complete, use a spray bottle to dampen the stitched area with cold water. Pull the waste canvas threads out one at a time with tweezers. It is easier to pull all the threads running in one direction first; then pull out the opposite threads. Allow the stitching to dry; then place face down on a towel and iron.

# Suppliers

All products are available retail from Shepherd's Bush, 220 24th Street, Ogden, UT 84401; (801) 399-4546; or for a merchant near you, write the following suppliers:

**Zweigart Fabrics**—Zweigart/Joan Toggitt Ltd., 35 Fairfield Place, West Caldwell, NJ 07006

Zweigart Fabrics used:
White Aida 14
White Aida 18
White Hardanger 22
Cream Hardanger 22
Black Hardanger 22
White Linda 27
Baby Pink Linda 27
White Belfast Linen 32
Cream Belfast Linen 32
Driftwood Belfast Linen 32
Floba 25
Terra Cotta Lugana 25
Rustico 14
Waste Canvas 14
Waste Canvas 16
Double Mesh White Canvas 20

**Glenshee Linen 29** (Pink, Gray, Blue)—Anne Powell Heirloom Stitchery, P.O. Box 3060, Stuart, FL 33495

**Jobelan** (Ivory, Tan)—Wichelt Imports, Inc., Rural Route 1, Stoddard, WI 54658

**Country Cloth 11**—Craft World, P.O. Box 779, New Windsor, MD 21776

**Christmas Fingertip Towels** (Rich Cranberry, Deep Teal)—Charles Craft, P.O. Box 1049, Laurinburg, NC 28352

**Beads**—MPR Associates, P.O. Box 7343, High Point, NC 27264

**Ribbon**—C. M. Offray & Son, Route 24, Box 601, Chester, NJ 07930-0601

**Rabbit Mat** (Blue, Pink)—Chappelle Designers, P.O. Box 9252, Newgate Station, Ogden, UT 84409

**Madeira Super Twist #30**—Beth's Stitching Post, 9842 Hibert St., Suite 233, San Diego, CA 92131

# Jacket Motifs

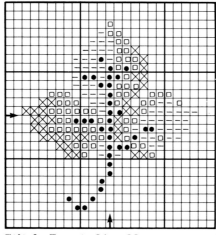

**Stitch Count: 21 x 22**

## Leaf

| Anchor | | DMC (used for sample) |
|---|---|---|
| | | **Step 1:** Cross-stitch (two strands) |
| 300 | – | 745 Yellow-lt. pale |
| 891 | □ | 676 Old Gold-lt. |
| 362 | ✕ | 437 Tan-lt. |
| 363 | ● | 436 Tan |

**Stitch Count: 21 x 21**

## Flowers

| Anchor | | DMC (used for sample) |
|---|---|---|
| | | **Step 1:** Cross-stitch (two strands) |
| 26 | – | 3708 Melon-lt. |
| 76 | ● | 962 Dusty Rose-med. |
| 86 | △ | 3608 Plum-vy. lt. |
| 87 | ∴ | 3607 Plum-lt. |
| 209 | □ | 913 Nile Green-med. |
| 189 | ✕ | 991 Aquamarine-dk. |

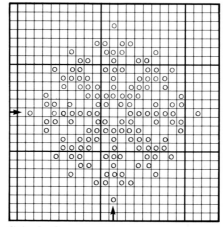

**Stitch Count: 21 x 21**

## Snowflake

| Anchor | | DMC (used for sample) |
|---|---|---|
| | | **Step 1:** Cross-stitch (two strands) |
| 1 | ○ | White |

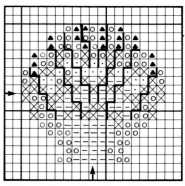

**Stitch Count: 17 x 16**

## Shell

| Anchor | | DMC (used for sample) |
|---|---|---|
| | | **Step 1:** Cross-stitch (two strands) |
| 926 | • | Ecru |
| 4146 | – | 754 Peach Flesh-lt. |
| 8 | ○ | 761 Salmon-lt. |
| 76 | ✕ | 962 Dusty Rose-med. |
| 42 | ▲ | 335 Rose |
| | | **Step 2:** Backstitch (one strand) |
| 897 | ⌐ | 221 Shell Pink-dk. |